RIGHT AND WRONG WAYS
TO USE THE BIBLE

J. CARTER SWAIM

RIGHT
AND
WRONG
WAYS
TO
USE
THE
BIBLE

PHILADELPHIA

THE WESTMINSTER PRESS

COPYRIGHT MCMLIII BY W. L. JENKINS

Library of Congress Catalog Number: 53–5959

PRINTED IN THE UNITED STATES OF AMERICA

TO

C. K. S.

συνκληρονόμος χάριτος ζωῆς

PREFACE

No age has had so many Bibles as our own. Bibles can be purchased now in drugstores, department stores, even five-and-tens. Numerous societies devote their energies to distributing copies free of charge.

The Bible in our time has been issued in many different formats. It has appeared in readable type and in print too fine for any but youthful eyes. It has appeared in bindings of red and blue, as well as in black covers that droop lugubriously over the edges. It has appeared in two-column pages and one-column pages, and with different versions side by side in parallel columns. It has appeared with verse numbers and without, in verse paragraphing and in paragraphing by sense.

The Bible is praised by almost everyone. Professors acclaim it as literature. Psychologists refer to it for illustrations of human behavior. Zionists use it as a guide in exploiting the resources of the Holy Land. Even agnostics tell us that no one can understand our society without a knowledge of the Bible.

Christians are constantly urged to read the Bible. Children in church school are encouraged to acquaint themselves with a few verses each day. Adults are given schemes by means of which they can get through the entire volume in a year. Ministers are sure that a great revival of religion would occur if only their people would read the Bible.

The truth is, however, that many who set out to read the Bible find it a discouraging enterprise. Some editions are, as books, the most unattractive ever encountered. Some versions are replete with unfamiliar words. All transport the reader to a land far away and a time long ago, a land of strange customs and a simple time difficult to comprehend by those who rush through doors opened by electric eyes, travel by jet plane, and spend their leisure with television.

Encountering unresolved difficulties of many sorts, the reader is apt to become discouraged. Since he has always been taught to look to the Bible for light and leading, inability to find it often leaves him with a sense of guilt. Sometimes he turns to a sect that promises all the answers. He thus transfers to others a responsibility that really is nontransferable.

Some of the common errors in Bible study need to be pointed out. The methods of true discernment need to be underlined. Hence this modest volume.

In its preparation I am conscious of being under obligation to many: parents and instructors of my youth; students and colleagues in the seminary; teachers and church officers enrolled in leadership training schools; pastors encountered at synods and conferences. The officers and members of many congregations have contributed more than they know. In particular I should like to mention the First Presbyterian Church of Staten Island, New York, and the Kingshighway Presbyterian Church, St. Louis, Missouri.

J. CARTER SWAIN.

Western Theological Seminary,
Pittsburgh, Pa.

CONTENTS

RIGHT AND WRONG WAYS
TO USE THE BIBLE

﴾ 1 ﴿

"HOW DO YOU READ?"

EXCEPT for sin, allegiance to the Bible is the only thing all Christians have in common. Jesus' followers differ regarding the proper procedures in worship. Some feel that set forms, worked out by earlier generations, are the only adequate expression of devotion. Others, cherishing the spontaneity of the Spirit, are sure that conventional molds can never be adequate. Christians differ regarding posture in prayer: some kneel, some stand, some sit. In *Life with Father* the contrast is drawn between Methodists and Episcopalians. Methodists do not get down on their knees so often as Episcopalians, but when they do get down they stay down longer!

Christians differ regarding the hymnbooks they use. Great hymns are the common property of Christendom, yet each denomination makes its own selection and arrangement. Christians differ regarding the sacraments. Some baptize infants; some baptize only those who have come to years of accountability. Some invite all believers to share with them in the Lord's Supper; some practice "close Communion." Some observe these two sacraments only; some insist that there are seven; others, that there is but one, the reading of the Word.

Christians differ in their interpretations of great doctrines: some believe in predestination; some do not. Some believe that it is not possible for a saved person to fall from grace; others have only too much evidence to support their belief in the possibility of backsliding. Christians differ in their understanding of religious obligation. Some are sure that it is a matter simply of inner piety; others, that it must show itself in social action. However Christians may differ in these matters, they are united in their conviction that the Bible is the authoritative book.

So accustomed are we to taking the Bible for granted that, spelled with a small " b," the very word has come to stand for the standard work in any field. Hilliard's *Greater Magic* has been called the magician's bible; the New York *Social Register,* the bible of the blue bloods; the *Sporting News,* baseball's bible; *Variety,* the bible of the show business; the works of Andreas Vesalius, the bible of anatomy. The Civil Defense Office of the National Security Resources Board has a 32-page pamphlet containing instructions to civilians as to how they should act in the event of an atom bomb raid. The brochure is entitled *John Citizen's Bible on Atomic Attack Protection.*

A student intent on demonstrating his belief that Christianity is not different from other faiths collected into one volume writings from most of the world's religions. The product is useful for a study of comparative religion; just here it is the title that interests us. What name did he give this compilation? " Source Book for Comparative Religion "? " Sacred Writings "? " Excerpts from Great Religions "? No. None of these would have had much appeal for the book-buying public. He called it *The Bible of the World* (ed., Robert O. Ballou. The Viking Press, Inc., 1939).

Another man, bent on proving that Christianity is just

" neo-Messianism," with nothing really to distinguish it from Judaism, edited a collection of what he called the ethical elements from the various parts of the Scripture, although only 30 of the 368 pages were devoted to the New Testament. He did not call it " An Ethical Scrapbook," nor " Judaeo-Christian Ethics," but *A Bible for the Liberal* (ed., D. D. Runes. Philosophical Library, Inc., 1946). It is doubtful whether anyone in the Western world would now dare to start a religion without reference to the Bible. Joseph Smith contended that the Book of Mormon was authoritative because it was the fulfillment and completion of the Biblical revelation. Mary Baker Eddy's *Science and Health* has a profusion of Biblical quotations, and Mrs. Eddy gave her followers, not a new literature, but a " Key to the Scriptures."

Churchmen come to the Bible not as to a masterpiece of world literature, but as to a book that has in a special sense a message for them. The Bible is read in this way by all sorts of Christian groups. Their differences, indeed, they base upon their reading of the Bible. It is appealed to by Trinitarians and Unitarians, High-Church Anglican and Southern Baptist, Catholic and Protestant, Quaker and Spiritualist, liberal and conservative, orthodox and neo-orthodox. It seems a fair assumption that the nearer Christians come to letting the Bible speak its message to them, the closer they will be drawn to one another.

The groups just enumerated are expected to use the Bible. To any careful observer of our time it is impressive to note how many other groups there are that make use of the Bible, often in ways that are wholly unexpected — and, it may be, wholly unjustified. The Bible is used by Governments on more than one continent: by American patriots and totalitarian fanatics; by men faced with the necessity of doing something about war, militarists and pacifists and sufferers of every description; by men caught up in economic controversy; by the National Association of Manufacturers and the C.I.O.; by apologists for capitalism, socialism, and Communism; by all parties in the social struggle — employers, employees, and conciliators; and by an assortment of other people — football coaches, snake handlers, and earnest, self-forgetting scholars.

When a lawyer came asking, " What shall I do to inherit eternal life? " Jesus referred him to the Scripture: " What is written in the law? " he asked. " How do you read? " (Luke 10:25 f.). Jesus invariably gave a slightly different twist to conventional truths. Here was a man familiar with the law, and Jesus turned him back upon what he had always known. In so doing, Jesus employed a familiar formula — with a difference! In introducing Scriptural quotations, a regular rabbinical formula was, " What do you read? " Jesus saw unfailingly that the " how " is always more important than the " what." He knew that it was desirable to " take heed what you hear " (Mark 4:24), but only he discerned that it is necessary also to " take heed . . . how you hear " (Luke 8:18).

So on this occasion he is interrogating his inquisitor not merely about the contents of his reading but about the manner of it. Does he read in order to confirm his prejudices, or to form his opinions? Does he read in order to confute his opponents, or to find out what and whom he ought to oppose? Does he read through the eyeglasses of tradition, everything colored by what the fathers taught, or does he read in the glad confidence that there is more light yet to break forth from God's holy Word?

There is certainly no dearth of people who read the Bible today. At least, there are enough Bibles in circulation so that all Christians could read it simultaneously. The urgent question for our age is not, "Do you read the Bible?" but, "How do you read?" A glance around the world suggests that people approach it from many different points of view and read it in many different ways, but usually in search of confirmation for accepted practices rather than in intense desire to hear what God the Lord will say.

It is at once evident that everybody wants the Bible to be on his side. This is true of Republicans, Democrats, and most of the minor political parties that emerge from time to time. We are told that men and women are increasingly unfamiliar with Holy Writ. Recent Presidential campaigns, however, do not show any diminution in its use. Alben Barkley told the National Democratic Convention that Revelations (as he is reported to have called it) 3:20 constituted "a superb call to service," not just to the nation, but in a special sense to the Democratic Party. President Truman frequently stated that his foreign policy was based on the Sermon on the Mount, and once interrupted a campaign speech to read to a West Virginia audience Matt. 6:5 f. This description of the hypocrites, he insisted, was a good picture of the way his opponents were behaving.

When Truman proposed a tax reduction of $40 per person, to be offset by higher taxes on corporations, Harold E. Stassen announced that the President had offered the voters forty pieces of silver as "a price for their betrayal of their own good judgment." Henry Wallace opened his ill-starred campaign for the Presidency by stating that it was his intention to raise "a Gideon's army." Adlai Stevenson accepted the Presidential nomination in a speech that quoted, with slight alteration, Matt. 26:42, and Dwight Eisenhower proclaimed quite early in the campaign that he was " not going to be put in a position that I personally am a Messiah."

What is true of political parties is true of Governments, both at home and abroad. Consider the uses to which the Bible was put during the war. Fifteen months after Pearl Harbor, Bible sales in the United States had gone up by more than 25 per cent. This was not entirely due to purchase by individuals. Uncle Sam himself was one of the largest buyers of Bibles. In October, 1946, the War Assets Administration announced that it had a million Bibles to be given away to any organization that would make worthy use of them. The Government had not acquired these Bibles for the sake of making Christians, or better Christians, out of its soldiers. The announcement ran, " Most of the Bibles, left over from the 11,000,000 purchased for morale purposes, . . . are of pocket size " (*The New York Times*, October 6, 1946).

The Army, then, uses the Bible as it uses Bob Hope, Rita Hayworth, and Marlene Dietrich — to build morale! This official distribution of Bibles no doubt contributed to the furtherance of the belief that the Bible is in a special sense the possession of the people of the United States of America or of the English-speaking peoples generally. A small book published in Canada asserts that " in the Great War the lands in which the Bible was a closed book, or its teaching forbidden, suffered most from the ravages of war, and went down to defeat. The English-speaking peoples of the world, a Christian civilization, were victorious, and immediately began to feed their vanquished enemies, clothe them, and sent medicine to heal their sicknesses. But most of all, Bible-starved Europe and Japan need the Bible."

The truth is that Europe was not " Bible-starved." As the threat of World War II drew on, people there continued to buy it. Kenneth Latourette relates that "in the very time when Hitler was consolidating his power in Germany, from 1933 to 1938, each year the sales of the Bible outstripped those of his own widely promoted book, *Mein Kampf,* by more than 200,000, and that the sales of the Bible in Germany rose from 830,000 copies in 1930 to 1,120,000 in 1939" (*Advance Through Storm,* page 105. Harper & Brothers, 1945). The British and Foreign Bible Society reported that its sales alone in Germany amounted in 1939 to 275,000, which was more than two and one half times its record of the previous year.

Poland, in a year of tragedy, almost equaled the German performance. From a total of 54,000 in 1938, sales in Poland in 1939 went to 135,000, precisely two and one half times the previous year's sales. In Belgium the totals for 1939 were nearly double those for 1938. To the east, Romania's total was somewhat more than twice that of the previous year, and the same was true of Hungary. Nor was this increase confined to Europe. In China 2,296,000 copies of the Bible were sold in 1938, with an increase of 10 per cent in 1939.

So great is the prestige of the Bible that even the Nazis wanted it on their side, and steps were taken to revise its contents to make it coincide with their philosophy. Lacking the hardihood to ban the Bible, Hitler and his apologists felt that the next best thing was to try to make it play into their hands. Accordingly, all those parts favorable to the Jews were eliminated. The Biblical doctrines of loyalty and sacrifice were distorted into injunctions to serve the German state. Passages that speak of meekness were expurgated, and the names of deities that figure in Nordic mythology replaced Hebrew names.

This attempt of the Nazis to make the Bible say what

they wanted it to say is one of the strangest tributes ever paid to the hold that the Scripture has upon mankind. To emphasize the supposed similarity between *Mein Kampf* and the Bible, the Reich League of Government Officials presented to Hitler on his birthday in 1936 a unique copy of his autobiography. Seven graphologists labored for eleven months to transcribe it by hand on 965 pages of leather parchment in the script of the medieval Bible.

When the United States for the first time in its history began to draft men before the nation was at war, the Army was eager to have it appear that the Bible sanctioned such procedure. General Hugh S. Johnson wrote a newspaper column entitled " Biblical Draft." Marshaling Scripture for his purpose, he cited the following: for registration of the whole adult population and classification as to its availability for military service, Num. 26:1 f.; for assignment of quotas, Num. 31:30; for a helpful list of exemptions from military service, Deut. 20:5-9.

Those opposed to the draft pointed out that the general had taken all his ammunition from the Old Testament, neglecting such New Testament injunctions as " Resist not evil " and " Overcome evil with good," and that even in the Old Testament there is a dire precedent against registration. II Samuel, ch. 24, relates that David carried out a military registration that turned up " in Israel . . . eight hundred thousand valiant men who drew the sword, and the men of Judah were five hundred thousand " (II Sam. 24:9). This was displeasing to God, who promptly " sent a pestilence upon Israel . . . and there died . . . seventy thousand men " (II Sam. 24:15).

Once the nation was committed to war, individuals within it reacted in strangely diverse ways to the Bible. A famous soldier of World War I was Sergeant Alvin York, who on one occasion killed 20 Germans and brought back 132 prisoners. York had always professed great faith in the Bible, and at the time he registered for the draft asked for exemption on the ground that he was a conscientious objector. He was inducted anyway, and his commanding officer persuaded him that the only way he could become a peacemaker was by fighting. After the war, York returned to his home community and became superintendent of the Bible school. When Hitler appeared on the horizon, York went up and down the land arguing for preparedness. He visited Army camps and told young soldiers how important it was to have faith, and that he had carried his Bible with him all during World War I, reading it in dugouts and front-line trenches.

Other Christians were sure that if they were to take the Bible seriously they would have to abstain from participation in war. Following the first use of the atomic bomb against human beings, *Life* magazine (August 20, 1945) ran an editorial in which it stated: " Our sole safeguard against the very real danger of a reversion to barbarism is the kind of morality that compels the individual conscience, be the group right or wrong. The individual conscience against the atomic bomb? Yes. There is no other way."

Most of those whose consciences forbade them to participate in war were motivated by what they believed the Bible to teach. They remembered that Israel found that " the war horse is a vain hope for victory and by its great might it cannot save " (Ps. 33:17), and that the prophet Zechariah (Zech. 4:6) said, " Not by might, nor by power, but by my Spirit, says the Lord of hosts." They were mindful of Jesus' promise that it was the peacemakers who should be called the children of God (Matt. 5:9), and of his warning, " All who take the sword will perish by the sword " (Matt. 26:52).

Two French pastors, who were Christian pacifists, got into trouble with the Vichy regime because of their insistence on taking care of Jewish refugee children. Thrown into a concentration camp, these men also read the Bible. Offered their release if they would pledge allegiance to the Petain Government, they refused. Their Communist fellow prisoners were intrigued that anyone in the modern world should refuse to sign a piece of paper if, by signing, he could gain his liberty. When they found out that it was the Bible that had given these two pastors that sense of honor, the Communists asked to sit in with the pastors in their Bible study.

As a result of what they learned, a spokesman for the Communists said: " We admit that your religion is superior to ours. This way of life that Jesus taught and lived is the way all men ought to live. It is the way all men will live — after the Revolution. But, of course, it isn't practical now " (quoted by A. J. Muste in *Not by Might*, pages xi f. Harper & Brothers, 1947).

Consider, again, how the Bible is appealed to by all parties to the economic strife that characterizes our age. The claim is not infrequently made that the Scripture ought to be read just because it will undergird this ideology or flatten that one. A member of the Roman hierarchy urged upon the people of the New York diocese daily Bible-reading as an antidote to Communism. An American clergyman who visited Russia reported that in the Greek Orthodox Church there had been a marked revival of Bible-reading. Archbishop Damaskinos explained that Bible-reading was being encouraged in order to combat Communism.

Louis Wallis wrote a book called *The Bible Is Human,* which contends that the Bible must now be interpreted as the book of democracy. Leading industrialists cite the Scripture in support of capitalism. Acting on the principle set forth in Matt. 25:14-30, an Ohio church one February Sunday gave each worshiper a ten-dollar bill, with the request that it be put to work for the Lord. By June the $2,000 originally distributed had grown to $9,573, and the story was front-page news in a publication of the National Association of Manufacturers. The parable was hailed as encouraging free enterprise, and the minister was lauded for having " summoned individual initiative " (*Understanding,* August, 1947).

It is likely that the mass of American church members would agree that the Bible is a bulwark of capitalism, but not all Christian thinkers would assent to that proposition. Walter Rauschenbusch, a serious student of Christianity, has indeed written, " The most important advance in the knowledge of God that modern man can make is to understand that the Father of Jesus Christ does not stand for the permanence of the capitalistic system " (*Christianizing the Social Order,* page 322. The Macmillan Company, New York, 1913). Certainly many members of the British Labor Party would claim the support of the Scripture for their socialist program. It is John Mark, they tell us, not Karl Marx, who determines their policies.

The Labor movement in Britain has been distinguished for the large number of religious people who have had a leading part in it. Many of its outstanding figures have been sons of clergymen or lay readers or even lay preachers. Ernest Bevin was a lay preacher of the Methodist Church. Upon his death in 1951 his ashes were interred in Westminster Abbey, an honor bestowed upon the memory of few statesmen since Gladstone. Sir Stafford Cripps was the first layman ever invited to preach at a regular service in St. Paul's Cathedral. His sermon, early in January, 1950, had for its theme "Personal Faith and Christian Action." " There is nothing that matters so much in the world today," he said, " as that we should get back to the standards Christ set for us in our public and in our private life."

Even the Communists seem bent on using the Bible for their own purposes. Communist-led Viet-Minh soldiers fighting against the French in Indochina were expected to carry a 50-page propaganda booklet referred to as the Communist bible. Czech refugees in Vienna reported that the State Office for Church Affairs in Prague was seeking to rearrange the Bible in such a way as to make it support Communism. They hoped to set Christ's teachings in such a light that pious Catholics, especially in the rural regions, would believe they were acting against the gospel if they resisted collectivist farm programs.

Not only is the Scripture quoted on the ideological front, but it figures from time to time in the strife between capital and labor. A feature story on the late William Green, head of the American Federation of Labor, held that in order to understand Green it was necessary to recall that he earned his first money, a five-dollar gold piece, by reading the whole Bible aloud to his illiterate father. At the A.F.L. convention held in San Francisco attention was given to the Taft-Hartley Act, which required anti-Communist affidavits of all labor union executives. John L. Lewis strode to the platform and shouted: "'Thou shalt not muzzle the ox that treadeth out the corn.' . . . I am reminded of the Biblical parable, 'Lions led by asses'" (*Time,* October 27, 1947).

The "muzzling the ox" passage is taken from Deut. 25:4, a humanitarian provision for animals, which Paul adapts to the Christian ministry (I Cor. 9:9 f.; cf. I Tim. 5:18). The "lions led by asses" is a little more difficult to identify. Since the Scripture is always true to nature and lions are never led by asses, this sounds more like Aesop's fables than like a story out of the Bible. This seems to be an illustration of the human tendency to attribute to the Bible every literary allusion that sticks in the memory. People have requested the Biblical location of such non-Biblical sayings as "God helps those who help themselves," "God tempers the wind to the shorn lamb," and "Know thyself."

Employers too find their uses for the Bible. The mediation board asked Quincy Beltram, of the International Edge Tool Company, Newark, New Jersey, why he had discharged 11 workers who had joined a C.I.O. union. He replied that he was following the Biblical exhortation, "Drive out a scoffer, and strife will go out." On his return to the plant, Beltram, who was accustomed to have daily Bible classes for his workers, found that the lessons had sunk in. Pickets greeted him with a sign on which they too had quoted from the Bible: "Masters, treat your slaves justly and fairly." Thereupon Beltram rehired the discharged employees and signed a union contract.

Canadian-born Cyrus S. Ching, former director of the Federal Mediation and Conciliation Service, was fond of citing Biblical parallels to modern labor troubles. He pointed out that there was not too much literature on the subject, but that one of the best studies was to be found in the fifth chapter of Exodus. "Pharaoh, the boss, in order to cut down expenses after suitable time studies had been made, said the boys would have to furnish their own straw to make bricks. Most of the straw had apparently been gathered by someone else and the quality of the bricks deteriorated. There was discussion also of the speed-up system and some reference was made to outside agitators. The sitdown strike had not come into vogue at the time, so there was a walkout" (*The New York Times Magazine*, October 26, 1947).

The strange ways in which the Bible enters into our common life are almost beyond imagining. Turning to the realm of sport, we find, improbably enough, that the Scripture continues to be cited. The backfield members of a famous football team were called " The Four Horsemen," in obvious reference to the Apocalypse (Rev. 6:2 ff.), although no indication was given as to which was white, which was red, which was black, which was pale. Cleveland's Browns, a professional football team, were accustomed under the leadership of Coach Paul Brown to huddle in the dressing room before a game, pray that they would be able to do their best and enjoy the competition, and conclude with the Lord's Prayer.

Football Coach Harvey John Harmon picked an all-Biblical football team that he would have liked to coach. He believed the following line-up would be effective: Abner, left end; Job, left tackle; Peter, left guard; Samson, center; Moses, right guard; Jacob, right tackle; Gideon, right end; David, quarterback and captain; Daniel, left half; Joshua, right half; John the Baptist, fullback.

In justifying these selections, Harmon offered the following explanation: " For center, Samson — he could take out all seven of the opposing linemen at once. For guards, Peter the Rock and Moses — Moses was so strong and able to take the gaff that I'd not only make him a guard but put him on the Football Rules Committee too. . . . For halfbacks: Joshua, of whom the Bible says that he 'passed through,' and Daniel, who was resolute and stuck to the right. I'd put Daniel in charge of the training table too: he showed he knew his simple fare was better than the pyorrhea-giving diet of the Babylonians. For fullback, John the Baptist — he'd prepare the way " (*Time*, February 8, 1937).

The examples thus far cited have been chosen from individuals and groups that made no special claim to being religious. If it is surprising to find the Scripture appealed to and quoted so frequently among them, it is even more astonishing to discover the uses to which the Bible has sometimes been put by those who claim that their lives are completely dominated by it.

In the little Georgia town of Euharlee, Rev. George Miller stood up to preach. Beside him was a box from which there came the unmistakable sounds of a rattlesnake. He quoted a passage from the King James Version: " They shall take up serpents; and if they drink any deadly thing, it shall not hurt them " (Mark 16:18).

So saying, he plunged his hand into the box and brought out two giant rattlers. Presently he brought out the " salvation cocktail," and said to one of those standing by, " Brother Davis, do you believe in the power of the Lord great enough to take what's in this bottle? " Ernest Davis, a thirty-four-year-old farmer, grabbed the glass, took several gulps — and five days later was dead of strychnine poisoning.

A charge of manslaughter was brought against the preacher, but was thrown out of court on the ground that there was no law to prevent an individual from carrying poison, and it had been testified that Miller said to Davis, " I warn you not to take it unless the Lord directs you to."

When the charge was dismissed, Miller clapped his hands and shouted, " If they don't believe I have the power of God, let them bring me a snake or some poison." He announced that there would be a big celebration Saturday night, at which, " if the Lord moves me, I will handle snakes and drink poison again " (*Time,* September 8, 1947; *Pittsburgh Post-Gazette,* September 12, 1947).

All this is eloquent of present-day confusion about the Bible, not only as to what it says but as to how we ought to go about learning what it means. Is the Bible Democratic, Republican, or third party? Does it teach capitalism, socialism, or Communism? Is it on the side of the workers, the owners, or the managers? Does its teaching about prayer extend to athletic contests? Does it encourage us to fly in the face of the laws by which the universe is run? Or is any of these the right question? Are we not wrong in bringing to it our presuppositions and merely seeking to find in it quotations to bolster our position?

Ought we not humbly and teachably to sit down before it and consider what God the Lord will say? It is related of a certain Scottish minister, Struthers of Greenock, that " he never read the Scripture as if he had written it: he always read it as if listening for a Voice " (Adam W. Burnet, *Pleading with Men,* page 102. Fleming H. Revell Company, 1935). This was no doubt said specifically of the public reading of Scripture, but it is of first importance for us all, whether in public or in private, to read God's Book " as if listening for a Voice."

2

"DO YOU UNDERSTAND WHAT YOU ARE READING?"

An official of the Abyssinian court was crossing the Syrian Desert, reading the scroll of the prophet Isaiah. In the manner of the Oriental, he was reading aloud. A Christian missionary overheard, and was so intrigued by the unusual circumstance that he approached the traveler and said, "Do you understand what you are reading?" (Acts 8:30). The missionary wanted to be sure that the sense of what he was reading was clear to the inquiring spirit. It is a good question. It is, indeed, the second point that confronts us when we think of how the Scripture ought to be used: "Do you understand what you are reading?"

There are religions in which it does not matter whether or not the worshiper understands the sacred books. In Islam there is a frank acceptance of a double standard in language. The common man cannot be expected to understand the holy writings. The fellahin who speak "low Arabic" are not acquainted with the "high Arabic" of the Koran. This does not matter, for it is believed that the hearer can somehow benefit simply by listening to the rhythmical chant of the words he does not understand. This produces upon the hearer an effect known as "lawful magic."

A men's Bible class spent the larger part of one Sunday morning session discussing the difference between "throughly" and "thoroughly." "Throughly," explained the teacher learnedly, "is not in the dictionary [he evidently did not have an unabridged], but it is in God's Word [cf. the King James Version at Gen. 11:3; Job 6:2; Ps. 51:2; Jer. 6:9; 7:5; 50:34], and so we have to try to understand it."

He called upon the various members of the group to expound the difference. None was prepared to do it, but that did not deter them from trying. The consensus seemed to be that "throughly" must mean through and through, while "thoroughly" might simply mean from end to end and from side to side. This distinction is nonsense, but the average church school teacher could hardly be expected to know that the two words are identical, "throughly" being just an archaic spelling of "thoroughly."

Discussions of this kind seem to be about on a level with the lawful magic of Islam. Certainly they are alien to the Hebrew-Christian tradition, which has always been careful that people should have the sacred writings in a language that they could understand. The synagogue of our Lord's time made such provision. The law was written in Hebrew, but in popular usage this language had been replaced by Aramaic. In the synagogue, the law continued to be read in Hebrew, but it had to be translated into Aramaic in order to be understood, and this was done portion by portion.

Bishop Neill, of the Anglican Church, tells of a colonel in the British Army who was held captive for many months in a Communist prisoner-of-war camp. Lacking any other literature, the officer gave thanks that at last there was time for him to do what he had always been urged to do and what he had always wanted to do, read the Bible for himself. To his great distress, this did not turn out to be the exhilarating experience he had been led to expect. He was not able to understand what he was reading. The vocabulary he did not understand, nor could he discern how the several parts could fit together.

This is a great pity, because the Bible has been from the beginning a book for the ordinary reader. Mark tells us (Mark 12:37) of one period in Jesus' ministry that "the great throng heard him gladly." This was during the last week of His life, and is spoken with regard to Jesus' encounters with the guardians of tradition. The authorities were seeking to trap him. First one question had been asked, then another. Each time Jesus replied in such fashion as to parry the intended blow. The interrogation, aimed at embarrassing him, was answered by him in such a way as to become an embarrassment to the propounders, with the result that "after that no one dared to ask him any question" (Mark 12:34).

Whereupon Jesus took the initiative and posed for them a question. Popular expectation held that Messiah would restore David's throne in a greater glory than Solomon's. The Messiah would necessarily be of the house of David. Citing Ps. 110:1, Jesus pointed out that David called the Messiah "Lord; so how is he his son?" This is the type of argument that was well understood at the time. It was the sort of casuistry in which the rabbis habitually engaged. Jesus met them on their own ground, and by their own methods cut that ground from under them. The people were immensely pleased. Thus it was that "the great throng heard him gladly."

On the Day of Pentecost a multitude gathered from every corner of the Mediterranean world exclaimed, "How

is it that we hear, each of us in his own native language? "
(Acts 2:8). Whatever their mother tongue, the common
people of every country heard gladly that day. Ever since,
the missionary has held that his first task was to give his
people the Book in a language they could readily comprehend.

Efforts to do this for English-speaking people reach back
into time almost as far as the beginnings of Anglo-Saxon
literature. The earliest poet known to us by name, Caed-
mon, was noted for his paraphrases of Bible stories. The
Venerable Bede, most famous scholar of his day in western
Europe, wrote an ecclesiastical history which is still a chief
source of knowledge of ancient England. As he lay on his
deathbed, Bede was dictating to his scribe a translation of
The Gospel According to John. " I don't want my boys to
read a lie," he said. Alfred the Great was eager that the
Scripture should be put into the rude speech of his fellows and hoped that every freeborn youth should learn to
read it well.

The first complete English translation did not appear
until about the year 1382. It was the work of John Wycliffe
and his colleagues. Wycliffe is known as the " Morning
Star of the Reformation." His version was made from the
Latin Bible of Jerome, and was therefore a translation of a
translation. The Hebrew and Greek originals were at that
time unknown to Christians. These were rediscovered in
the Renaissance, and the first complete English translation planned to be made from them was that of William
Tyndale, whose New Testament appeared in 1525. Tyndale was martyred for his pains. His dying words were,
" Lord, open the king of England's eyes! "

God did open the eyes of England's king, and in 1535
there appeared a translation bearing the name of Miles

Coverdale. Coverdale was Tyndale's friend and co-worker. The second edition of his work, appearing in 1537, bore on the title page, "Set forth with the Kynges moost gracious licence." The work of Tyndale and Coverdale found a fresh incarnation in the "Bible of the largyest volume," or Great Bible, which was issued in 1539 and has come to be known as the first authorized English Bible. The Geneva Bible, brought to America by the Pilgrims, appeared in 1560, and the Bishops' Bible in 1568. The latter was the second authorized version, and the King James Bible, of 1611, the third.

The next authorized version was the English Revision of 1881–1885, with its transatlantic variant, the American Standard Version of 1901. The fifth authorized Bible is the Revised Standard Version, the New Testament portion of which was published in 1946 and the entire Bible in 1952. This list of official Bibles indicates that English-speaking people have recognized the fact that, since their language is itself constantly changing, finality is not to be looked for in versions, but that translation is a labor that must be done afresh for each succeeding age.

In addition to the official versions of Scripture, a great many individuals have made their own translations. These have no other authorization than the right of the individual to interpret Scripture for himself. One of the most influential Bibles the English-speaking world has ever known was the Geneva Bible, issued in 1560 by the Protestants who, exiled from their own country, had found refuge in the city of John Calvin. The first English Bible to adopt verse divisions, this translation was provided with maps, tables of weights, measures, distances, etc., woodcuts, metrical psalms, and other aids to worship and study.

Published at a price that increased the range of possible

purchasers, it leaped at once into popularity. Almost 200 editions were called for before it ceased to be published in England, and approximately 150,000 copies were imported from Holland by Britishers after their own publishers ceased to carry it. For two generations this was the household Bible of Britain. It was the Bible of Cromwell's army, of the Scottish Covenanters, of the Pilgrim Fathers. Yet the only authority this Bible ever had was that of scholarly translators whose work met with a popular response. Did it need any other? Would it have been any better, or more effective, if it had borne a monarch's stamp of approval?

Our age is notable for the large number of unofficial, or private, translations that have been made. Those of Weymouth, Ballentine, and Mrs. Montgomery are but a few of the New Testament. One of the best known is called "An American Translation." This includes the Old Testament version prepared under the editorship of J. M. Powis Smith and the New Testament of Edgar J. Goodspeed. The Berkeley version of the New Testament was made by Gerrit Verkuyl. The first book translated into Basic English was the New Testament, and the whole Bible has been published in that limited vocabulary.

In addition to translations of the New Testament or the entire Bible, versions have been made of separate portions. During World War II, after his church had been destroyed by bombs, an English vicar completed in a bomb shelter his version of that part of the New Testament which is made up of letters. J. B. Phillips' *Letters to Young Churches* has been a popular volume. J. W. C. Wand, bishop of London, has his own version of the same portions of the Bible. He calls it *New Testament Letters; Prefaced and Paraphrased.* Edward Vernon published in 1952 *The*

Gospel of St. Mark: A New Translation in Simple English from the Nestle Greek Text.

The work of Bible translation is carried on by all sections of the Church. It is not the activity of those holding any one theological position. It is not a question at issue between liberals and conservatives. In 1937, Charles B. Williams issued what he called *The New Testament — A Translation in the Language of the People.* That version has been taken over by the Moody Bible Institute, and the edition of 1950 bears the imprint of The Moody Press. The publisher's preface states that "many evangelical Christians have wished for a modern, easy-reading translation prepared by a scholar who believes, as they do, that the entire Bible is the Word of God. The publishers are happy to be able to present this volume in answer to that long-felt need."

One of the best of the private translations is that of James Moffatt. A man of prodigious learning, Dr. Moffatt takes his place with Jerome, Tyndale, and Luther among the few men in history who have ventured to translate both the Hebrew Old Testament and the Greek New Testament. Dr. Moffatt was a Scottish Presbyterian who served sixteen years in the pastorate before becoming a theological teacher and who ended his life as a Church history professor in America. Those who are acquainted with the Scottish temperament will understand that Dr. Moffatt's background and heritage have fitted him in a peculiar way to enter into the mood and catch the undertones of the Biblical writers. So popular has this version been that a concordance to it has been issued, containing between 50,000 and 60,000 references.

Many matters of English literary style are clarified when we look into the present-day-speech versions. The King

James Bible did not use quotation marks, because that printer's device had not then been invented. In the old manuscripts, of course, there are no quotation marks either, so that the use of them now implies editorial decision. It is not always easy, as in John, ch. 3, to decide where quotation marks ought to go. Who can be quite sure where Jesus stops speaking and the Evangelist begins his commentary? It must be noted too that all those Testaments that print the words of Jesus in red also reflect some editor's judgment as to where the Saviour's own words begin and end.

Italic type is a device that the printer ordinarily employs for emphasis. A theological student said he had always been led to believe that the italicized words in the King James Bible were the most important. A look at some of them is confusing. Such words as " his," " is," " against," " her," " their," " one," etc., appear in italics in contexts where to emphasize them would be ridiculous. The King James translators followed a practice entirely different from our own. They put into italics words that were not in the original but which they considered necessary for proper English idiom. So far from being the most important words, then, they are words that were inserted by the translators!

Modern translators have abandoned this practice on the ground that if the insertion of a word is necessary to good English idiom, then it is implicit in the original. They really are not inserting anything but simply helping us to see what may be implied by the grammar or inflection of the Hebrew or Greek. Moffatt uses italics in yet another way, that is, to indicate New Testament passages that are quotations from the Old Testament.

The pun has been described as the lowest form of humor, yet it can be an effective device for fixing a truth in the memory. Where we might not recall a man's philosophical argument, we shall not forget his play on words. The Old Testament prophets frequently used this device, and often felt that they had solved everything if only they could sum it up in a neat phrase. Jesus too sometimes used the play on words. This may come as a surprise to many, for the reason that no puns appear in conventional English versions. The reason for this is that puns are exceedingly difficult to translate. Words in different languages do not have precise equivalents, and a play on words is the translator's despair.

It is one merit of Dr. Moffatt's version that he makes a valiant effort to preserve this Biblical usage. He has indeed a remarkable flair for doing so.

For instance, older versions tell us that Isaiah named one of his sons Maher-shalal-hash-baz (Isa. 8:1, 3 f.). " For before the child knows how to cry ' My father ' or ' My mother,' the wealth of Damascus and the spoil of Samaria will be carried away before the king of Assyria." The explanation, when translated into English, doesn't explain. The name was intended to symbolize the speedy destruction which the king of Assyria would inflict upon the allied kings Pekah and Rezin. Moffatt preserves the full significance by translating the wordplay: " Name him ' Spoil-soonpreyquick.' For before the boy knows how to say, ' my father ' and ' my mother,' the wealth of Damascus and the spoils of Samaria shall be carried off to the king of Assyria." In Hos. 1:6-9, Moffatt enables us to understand why Hosea gave his children the names he did. So also with place names. " The city of David " he renders " David's burg," and the place where Samson carried out one of his exploits was named " Jawbonethrow " (Judg. 15:17).

In John 21:15 f. English versions generally obscure a significant distinction by using a single English word for two entirely different Greek terms. The King James Version has it: "Feed my lambs. . . . Feed my sheep." The Revised Standard has: "Feed my lambs. . . . Tend my sheep." Yet "tend" is a noncommittal word that might be used of anything from babies to furnaces. The Greek word here is a distinctive term characteristic of Biblical imagery. Moffatt preserves it: "Feed my lambs. . . . Be a shepherd to my sheep."

In John 17:12 the usual rendering is, "None of them is lost but the son of perdition." Moffatt, however, finds cognate English terms for rendering the cognate Greek ones: "Not one perished — only the son of perdition." John 20:27 contains two words of which one is the negative of the other. The usual translations miss this: "Be not faithless, but believing." Admittedly, it is difficult to find cognate English terms that suggest the contrast found in the Greek, but Moffatt comes up with "Be no more unbelieving but believe."

Some of the new translations give helpful introductory matter. *The Twentieth Century New Testament,* by placing Mark first among the Gospel writers and the Thessalonian letters at the beginning of Paul's correspondence, dramatizes the fact that the order of Biblical books in the old manuscripts was subject to considerable variation. The attempt is made in this version to arrange the books, within the several categories, in the order of their composition, as nearly as that can be determined. Although not in the conventional order, the Gospels are still first. If the historical order were really to be preserved, the letters of Paul would come before the four Gospels. Many helpful insights come to one who reads the Biblical books in the approximate order of their origin.

Objection is sometimes made to new translations on the ground that to abolish archaic phrases tends to cheapen the Scripture. One lady wrote, " Let the Holy Word alone, in its quaint phraseology and matchless style." It is wrong, we are told, to put high and holy things into commonplace words. But that is precisely what our Lord and his apostles did. The New Testament represents their expression of eternal truth in the simple everyday words that could be understood by the common people. In order, therefore, to retain the true flavor of the New Testament, we must have it in the living language of our time.

One lady asked whether the new translations were not " destroying the reverence of the Bible." It is difficult to know exactly what she meant, but the proper answer seems to be: " If ‘ reverence ’ obscures truth, then ‘ reverence ’ needs to be destroyed. It is not recorded in Scripture that God's people perished for lack of reverence. They did perish for lack of knowledge. We must not allow any false ideas of ‘ reverence ’ to rob us of the knowledge that saves the soul." If we are not able to understand what we read, then we are on the level of Islam's lawful magic.

Another aspect of this matter is important. Protestants are not the only ones who have found out that the Bible needs to be put into language people can understand. In August, 1950, about 100,000 persons from 67 countries gathered in New York for the international assembly of Jehovah's Witnesses. The meetings were held in Yankee Stadium, with larger crowds present than Babe Ruth ever drew. A feature of that convention was the presentation of what was called the *New World Translation of the Christian Greek Scriptures.*

For some reason Jehovah's Witnesses do not choose to

call it the New Testament, but that is what it is. It is a translation that has its own peculiarities, and its own excellences too. The Witnesses, who are enthusiastic in the spread of their tenets, regard this as one of their most effective devices. A young Protestant clergyman in an Ohio town answered a knock at the door. It was a member of the sect, with a copy of this new version. " Your Church," said the Witness, " has not had a new translation of the Bible in over three hundred years; take this one and study it." The man was mistaken, of course, and the young minister took pride in showing him a copy of the Revised Standard Version.

The Roman Catholic Church also has chosen to give the people the Scripture in a language they can understand. During the past decade there have been at least three new English translations offered with the approval of the hierarchy. There is a Papal Biblical Commission that sponsors and supervises these projects. In some European countries too the Roman Catholic Church is issuing fresh translations. We have thought that this Church was trying to keep the Bible from the people, but that is no longer officially the case. A ruling of the pope now makes it possible for an individual to get an indulgence of three hundred days by reading the Scripture for fifteen minutes in an approved translation — and this can be obtained every day.

Ministers presumably acquire in theological seminary ability to make their own translations of Scripture, but many of them have even found present-day-speech versions helpful. A quarterly journal conducted a symposium in which each of 25 ministers listed the 10 books that had influenced him the most. First on the list of a prominent Congregational minister was Moffatt's Translation, of which he said that it " colloquially brings home the availability of the energy God poured through Jesus" (*Religion in Life,* autumn, 1950). Another contributor to the symposium listed Weymouth's Translation, stating that to him it was the most satisfying version. Several published sermons of the late Peter Marshall take their texts from Moffatt or Goodspeed. "Get a good modern translation," he used to tell his congregations.

He who cannot use the original languages of Scripture would do well to surround himself with as many translations as possible. Miles Coverdale, maker of the first English Bible issued with official approval, said in the preface to his work, "Sure I am that there cometh more knowledge and understandinge of the Scripture by their sondrie translacyons than by all the gloses of oure sophisticall doctours." To this day it remains true that for the ordinary student of the Bible one of the best aids is a variety of versions. Only thus can an affirmative answer be given to the question, "Do you understand what you are reading?"

There is, of course, in Philip's question an even deeper significance. He is asking not merely, "Is the vocabulary such as you can grasp?" but also: "Do you get the full import of this? Does it disclose to you what it intends to reveal about God?" New translations are often of value in disclosing meanings that before had been hidden or passed over.

A policeman in the State of Washington followed a motorist at forty-five miles an hour over a stretch of road that had on it nine signs reading: "Slow. Curve." "Speed 20 miles per hour," etc. The motorist paid no attention to any of the signs. When the patrolman finally overtook him and asked if he could not read, he said, "I've driven that road twice a day for fifteen years, and there are no signs on it." When the officer took him back and showed him some of them, he insisted that they must have been put up the night before! It is possible for human beings to become so familiar with signs along the Way that they overlook them entirely. Fresh translations serve to bring them sharply to attention.

Robert Louis Stevenson once said that he wished that he had never read the New Testament. The Methodist theologian Edwin Lewis, of Drew University, is on record as having said something similar. He wished that he had never read the New Testament. This seems a strange thing for these men to be saying, and they surely cannot have meant by it what Gamaliel Bradford meant when he said that he wished he had never read it. " I do not dare to look at the New Testament," he declared, "for fear of its awakening a storm of anxiety and self-reproach and doubt and dread of having taken the wrong path, of having been traitor to the plain and simple God " (quoted in *Younger Churchmen Look at the Church*, page 249, edited by R. H. Read. The Macmillan Company, 1935).

Stevenson and Lewis wished they had never read it for the reason that they would like to be able to come to it afresh and let it make upon them the impression it would make upon somebody who had not known it before. That is not a possibility for any of us. The Book has entered too much into our thought, too much into our vocabulary, although, alas, not enough into our lives. The next best thing to coming to the Scripture as if we never had read it is for us all a possibility. All we need to do is to read it in one or more of the new translations which have been a happy characteristic of Biblical scholarship in the past half century.

3

" DO YOU KNOW GREEK? "

PAUL in Jerusalem had been arrested, charged, among other crimes, with taking an uncircumcised Ephesian into the Temple, past the barrier beyond which Gentiles were not supposed to go. Brought before a Roman official, Paul asked if he could say a word. The magistrate, mistaken as to Paul's identity, was surprised at the tongue used by the prisoner. " Do you know Greek? " he asked. " Are you not the Egyptian, then, who recently stirred up a revolt and led the four thousand men of the Assassins out into the wilderness? " (Acts 21:37, 38).

Whereupon Paul made it clear that he was neither an Egyptian nor a dagger man, but " a Jew, from Tarsus in Cilicia." He had spoken in Greek because Greek was the universal language of the time, used by educated men in most of the regions where Alexander the Great had scattered his culture. It is notable that Paul addressed the Roman magistrate, not in Latin, but in Greek. Marcus Aurelius, the Roman emperor from A.D. 161 onward, composing his *Meditations*, did so, not in the language of the old Romans, but in the widespread language of culture, Greek.

Thus it came about that the New Testament, although

principally written by men of Hebrew background, was composed in the Greek language and found ready acceptance throughout the Mediterranean world. The Fourth Evangelist, writing, no doubt, for people outside Palestine, explains that, at the crucifixion of Jesus, the accusation inscribed above the cross was written " in Hebrew, in Latin, and in Greek " (John 19:20). Hebrew (or Aramaic) was the language of contemporary Palestine; Latin was the language of the conquerors; Greek was the language of civilized men everywhere. The writer of the Fourth Gospel probably saw in this a symbol of the universal significance of Christ.

Those three languages have all profoundly influenced Christianity. The Old Testament was written in Hebrew, the New Testament in Greek, while a Latin translation of both was the only Bible known to the Middle Ages. It would be interesting to explore the influence of the Vulgate upon Christian theology, and a specialist in Old Testament studies must understand an Oriental tongue which reads, not from left to right, but from right to left! We must here confine ourselves to the New Testament and to the magistrate's inquiry, " Do you know Greek? " It is a good question, and might be directed to each of us.

The popular saying, " It's all Greek to me " (a perversion of *Julius Caesar*, Act I, Scene 2, line 288), reveals plainly that most of us do not know Greek. Perhaps, however, there are more people than we realize who do have such knowledge. Of Bishop Ridley, burned at the stake in the days of Mary, Roger Williams said that he " had got most of the holy Epistles in Greek by heart." That was in the sixteenth century and may not surprise us. Even among our contemporaries, however, familiarity with the Greek Testament is an accomplishment not unknown.

There is an elderly woman in Pittsburgh, a Vassar College graduate, who regularly reads her Greek Testament, often carrying it with her on the streetcar.

Reading the Greek dramatists in the original is said to be a favorite diversion of Branch Rickey, and his religious interests make it likely that the baseball magnate also reads his New Testament in Greek. When Jan Christiaan Smuts, the South African statesman, died, his obituary stated that when he rode with his troops in the Boer War he carried a copy of Kant's *Critique of Pure Reason* and a Greek Testament in his saddlebag. A college teacher in Seattle said she was engaged in reading the Greek Testament and comparing it with French and German translations — always a rewarding exercise for the linguist.

Dorothy L. Sayers wrote for the BBC a cycle of twelve plays on the life of Christ. These were professionally produced by Val Gielgud, and have been published in this country under the title *The Man Born to Be King*. A writer of mystery stories has been captured by the supreme mystery. A creator of drama has caught something of the cosmic import of the divine-human encounter that once transpired in Palestine. A storyteller has given new winsomeness to the old, old story. The secret of Miss Sayers' effectiveness seems to be nothing less than this: she has read the Greek Testament for herself and has learned, as New Testament writers originally did, to have Jesus speak in the living language of the common people: "Happy are the sorrowful, for their souls are made strong through suffering." "There are many inns on the road to my Father's house. I am going to prepare the lodgings for you."

An elderly woman wrote to her favorite newspaper about the joys she had had in life. She was in her seventies, and because of reduced income could no longer travel; she had therefore to content herself with elemental things. One was the heavens at night. " Henry Dill Benner," she said, " has taught me to look up at the stars. So I have bought a simple book on astronomy." Another was poetry. Another was the memory of a sister " who made this home a little heaven for many years." Then there was the New Testament in the original. " I have Saint John's Gospel in Greek," she wrote. " I wonder if my Greek teacher knows that, after sixty years, I remember the joy I had in his classes. Sad I sometimes am; bored I can never be."

It is interesting to note in this connection that St. John's College, famous for its " Great Books " curriculum, announced in 1949 that it had dropped Latin in favor of two years of Greek. Previously it had taught one year of each. Latin was abandoned on the theory that a year was not sufficient to give comprehensive instruction in either language, and Greek was considered to offer the better background for general purposes.

The Greek Orthodox Church has petitioned the World Council of Churches to make Greek one of the official languages of the ecumenical movement. The argument is that not only is it used by that branch of Christendom, but also much of early theology was written in it, and that it is the original language of Christianity. American participation in world affairs has confronted some of our citizens with the realization that Greek is still a living language. The average Christian knows only of two letters *to* Thessalonians. Students at a theological seminary recently saw a letter *from* Thessalonians.

Chrysoula Sakale wrote to a Pennsylvania woman to express thanks for dresses that had been received. In words remarkably like those of II Tim. 4:13, she asked for warm clothing as protection against the rigors of winter. The letter was written by a Christian woman, and in it were a number of distinctly Biblical words. In the close-knit world of the twentieth century, the world of ECA and the Marshall Plan, the original language of the New Testament helps to give insights into the minds and hearts of Europeans who even now are the recipients of our benevolence, as well as the objects of our political concern.

There died some years ago in our nation's largest city one Osmund Phillips, who was assistant managing editor of *The New York Times*. Editors maintain astonishing anonymity until they die, but in his obituary a great deal was made of the fact that this man of business and journalism had a background of classical learning. The study of the Greek language had been his hobby, and he had devoted the leisure of all the last years of his life to making for himself an English translation of the Greek Testament. No doubt every minister could wish for a churchful of people who would do just that — each make his own version of the Greek Testament.

The fresh study of the Greek Testament has always brought enrichment to the life of the Church. Constant reference to the original is the only safeguard of Biblical truth. The Protestant Church is committed to vernacular versions of the Scripture, but popular speech changes so swiftly and drastically that there is continual need for return to the source of Biblical ideas. Nobody has been more keenly aware of this than Martin Luther. The Reformation began, indeed, when Martin Luther discovered that the Greek Testament did not say, " Do penance," but rather, " Change your mind " — that is, repent. The first of Luther's ninety-five propositions was nothing more nor less than this.

For most men and women, however, reading the Greek Testament is not now a possibility. A Pittsburgh lawyer relates that he studied Greek in high school, but there are some colleges where courses in it are seldom offered. Some institutions have substituted courses in " civilization " for a study of the original languages of civilization. When the Pilgrim Fathers set out from Leyden, old John Robinson told them that there was more light yet to break forth from God's holy Word. Those who read it in the original are particularly apt to find this light breaking upon them. If we cannot do that, we must trust somebody to translate it for us. Scholars are better able to do this now than ever before.

Students of classical Greek — Plato, Aristotle, Thucydides — once looked down upon New Testament Greek, somewhat like those Missouri schoolteachers who reputedly took " Dizzy " Dean to task for the poor English he used in broadcasting baseball games. To those accustomed to dealing with the work of the philosophers and historians, New Testament Greek seemed barbarous and slovenly. We now know why that was, and are not ashamed of it. We know that God spoke through the hearts and tongues and pens of common men.

It is only within the past half century that men have been able really to understand the special character of New Testament Greek. Not only does it differ from classical Greek, but it differs even from the literary Greek of its own period. Plutarch, the Greek biographer and moralist, lived a life that almost exactly spanned the period of the creation of the New Testament. Plutarch wrote in conscious imitation of the Attic writers of the classical period.

Various explanations had been offered as to why New Testament Greek differed from classical. One was that it was a special dialect of the Holy Spirit. Another was that it was Jewish Greek. That is to say, the men who gave us the New Testament were, for the most part, steeped in the traditions, the thought-forms, and the vocabulary of the Hebrews, so that even when they used the Greek language they continued to think in Aramaic. Anyone who thinks in English and writes in German will not write good German. So men who thought in Hebrew sometimes wrote poor Greek.

There no doubt are Hebraisms in the New Testament. " I am the way, and the truth, and the life," for example, is probably a Hebraism for " I am the true and living way." In the third century B.C. the Old Testament had actually been translated into Greek by scholars at Alexandria, and this helped to fix the vocabulary of the New Testament writers. In some instances the evidence for this kind of influence is so strong that some scholars have supposed that the documents were first written in Aramaic and then translated into Greek. No Aramaic original, however, has ever turned up.

The true key to our knowledge of the popular language of our Lord's time arises out of the discovery in recent decades of a great number of documents that date from approximately the period of the New Testament. These documents are not literary, but are of a completely casual nature: bills of sale, letters from fathers to their sons, notices of public meeting, wills, receipts, petitions, etc. These were never intended to be literature. They were written to be read once and thrown away — and they were thrown away!

They have been found on the dump heaps outside old Egyptian towns, and have survived only because the warm sands and salubrious climate of Egypt have preserved even the fragile writing materials of antiquity, frail papyrus leaves. "Papyrus" is the word from which we get the English "paper." The plural is "papyri," and these documents are known as nonliterary papyri. Their authors had no literary ambitions, and were not in the least concerned with the imitation of classical models. They simply expressed routine ideas in the language in which they regularly set forth the thoughts and activities of the daily round.

The remarkable thing about these nonliterary papyri is that their Greek is the same as that of the New Testament: its verb forms, its vocabulary, its want of literary style. All this means that the New Testament was written, not in the language of the philosopher, the schoolroom, or the lecture hall, but the language of the street corner, the market place, and the fireside. Celsus, one of the early critics of Christianity, ridiculed what he called the "sailor style" of the Gospels, but we now rejoice that Jesus' words were not recorded in classical Greek, where they would be accessible only to the learned, but in the everyday speech of the common man.

We may even credit Celsus with true discernment. Fishermen played a leading part in the events that led to the creation of the New Testament, and some of its vocabulary is such as would be readily understood by sailors. When Jesus said, "You are the salt of the earth" (Matt. 5:13), he was addressing fishermen who were in a better position than anyone else to appreciate the saving significance of salt. Lacking modern techniques of refrigeration, the fisherman knew that salt alone could preserve his catch. In Luke 5:5, Peter says, "Master, we toiled all night and took nothing!" The Greek word translated "Master" is found only in Luke and is different from the word similarly translated in Luke 5:8. It is really a sailor's word: "Captain."

Many passages have become more vivid as a result of increasing knowledge about the special character of New Testament Greek. It has long been commonplace that "the Jews have no dealings with the Samaritans" (John 4:9, K. J. V.). This is simply not true. There was hostility between them, but in post-Exilic Judaism trade could be carried on with heathen (cf. Neh. 13:16). The story as it appears in John's Gospel carries on the face of it a denial of the assertion that Jews and Samaritans had nothing to do with each other. The reason Jesus was resting by the well was that "his disciples had gone away into the city to buy food" (John 4:8). The Greek verb here really means "associate familiarly." Jews and Samaritans had no intimate dealings, but this did not preclude business transactions. Race prejudice is seldom allowed to interfere when it is a question of making a profit.

Judas served as treasurer of the apostolic band, and the older versions said that he "had the bag," an expression that has become a part of the popular idiom. It is now known, however, that what Judas carried was not a bag but a money box. The prodigal son did not simply gather all together, as the familiar translations render it. What he did was to realize on everything, turning it into cash, in the hope that he could take it with him. Older versions tell us that Paul, in addressing the Thessalonians, had heard that some of them were walking "disorderly" (II Thess. 3:11). We now know that the word means "playing truant." They were not going to work; they were loafing.

The "tables" served by the deacons (Acts 6:2) were not long dining tables, as is often supposed. These were not in use among the Hebrews. The tables referred to are those used by money-changers. The expression therefore means " attend to money matters " or " keep books." Older versions have the Pharisee claiming to " give tithes of all that I possess " (Luke 18:12). A man was not required to tithe his capital. If he did that, his contribution as well as his resources would become continually less. The Greek here means " all that I get," so that the Pharisee is telling us that he tithes his income rather than his possessions.

Translators formerly told us that when Jesus was crucified Pilate " gave the body to Joseph " (Mark 15:45). The Greek implies a little more than that. Pilate was in a position to demand a money payment. Instead, he asked no bribe but simply " granted the body to Joseph." A serious chronological difficulty is removed by knowledge of the special character of New Testament Greek. Matthew 28:1 (K. J. V.) tells us that " in the end of the sabbath " the women came to the tomb. The Jews counted the day from sunset to sunset. The sabbath ran from sunset on Friday to sunset on Saturday. " In the end of the sabbath " would therefore be late on Saturday afternoon.

This is not the time indicated by the other Evangelists, all of whom are agreed that the resurrection took place on the morning of the first day of the week. When the King James Bible was made, the Greek phrase that occurs here was not known to have any other meaning than " in the end of the sabbath." Recent discoveries make it clear that Matthew is not really mistaken in his chronology. The phrase ought to be translated, " After the sabbath." Thus the Gospels no longer tell different stories about the date of the resurrection.

A Bible student working on a manuscript was puzzled as to the hour of the day when Jesus died. There were no clocks in Bible times, and the hours of daylight were divided into twelve portions. Each of these was an " hour," though it is obvious that these hours would seldom have exactly sixty minutes. The amount of daylight varies in Palestine, as elsewhere. Mark 15:33 says, " And when the sixth hour had come, there was darkness over the whole land until the ninth hour." The sixth hour is the middle of the day, or noon. The ninth hour is the middle of the afternoon, or approximately 3 P.M.

Present-day-speech versions are right when they translate these terms into our current usage. Moffatt says, " When twelve o'clock came, darkness covered the whole land till three o'clock." Goodspeed has it, " At noon darkness spread over the whole country, and lasted until three in the afternoon."

It is desirable also that Greek terms of measurement, whether of distance or of coinage, be translated into the familiar idiom. Older versions used the cubit as a measure of distance. On the postresurrection morning the disciples were in a little boat " not far from land, but as it were two hundred cubits " (John 21:8). How far was that? We can figure it out if we know how far one cubit was, but how far was that? Our English word " cubit " is the Latin *cubitum*, which means " elbow " or " forearm." Lacking yardsticks and tapelines, primitive man measured by such devices as were available: the span, the foot, the forearm. A cubit is the distance from the elbow to the tip of the middle finger. Since people's arms are by no means all the same length, this would be variable, but it is approximately 18 inches, and 200 cubits would be 300 feet. That is a laborious way of figuring it out, and the Revised Standard Version is much more readily understood: " About a hundred yards." Nobody can mistake that: it is the length of a football field.

The King James Version says of the Holy City that the measure of its wall is "a hundred and forty and four cubits" (Rev. 21:17). Moffatt is more readily grasped: "He made the measure of the wall seventy-two yards." The city itself was to be, in each dimension, "twelve thousand furlongs" (Rev. 21:16, K.J.V.). "Furlong" is compounded of "furrow" and "long"; Webster says that it is the length of the furrow in an ordinary field, "theoretically the side of a square containing ten acres." This comes out to one eighth of a mile. The term is still employed by surveyors and in title deeds, but is not in popular use, and Moffatt's "fifteen hundred miles" is much more intelligible.

In order to convey the proper sense, also, Greek terms having to do with coins ought to be translated into the current vocabulary. There is a story about an illiterate minister who was fond of describing miserly men as being "as stingy as Caesar." His perplexed parishioners once asked what he meant by this comparison. He replied that it was Biblical, that Jesus had said, "Bring me a penny," and when they brought it he asked: "Whose subscription is this? And they said, Caesar's" (a garbled version of Mark 12:15 f.). The Revised Standard's "inscription" makes the passage less confusing than "superscription," but in any case "penny" is misleading. The Greek word describes a silver coin, not a copper one. Since the money value in this instance was of no particular significance, some translators simply render it "coin." Goodspeed transliteratis the word into "denarius." Moffatt and Weymouth, using British terms, render it "shilling." Perhaps "quarter" or "half dollar" would best convey the sense to American ears.

The King James Version speaks of a poor widow who "threw in two mites, which make a farthing" (Mark

12:42). Neither "mite" nor "farthing" is a term in common use among us. In seventeenth century England a mite was one twenty-fourth of a penny, a farthing one fourth of a penny. The King James translators therefore were mathematically wrong in saying that two mites make a farthing. They were practically correct, however, for that was the nearest equivalent in the coinage of their day for the money units mentioned in the Greek. There are no coins among us quite so small and insignificant as those. It is desirable that we try to find, as the King James translators did, the nearest equivalents in the currency of our time. The Revised Standard Version has, "Two copper coins, which make a penny," a circumlocution to get around the fact that we have no coin smaller than a penny. Translating for contemporary Britishers, Moffatt has, "Two little coins, amounting to a halfpenny."

A large unit of currency in New Testament vocabulary is transliterated into English as "talent." We forget that this word originally signified a sum of money. Our use of it to express a gift of personality or native endowment is a derived use, and one that has been given the world by our Lord's story. It was the term used of the weight of a sum of silver. Moffatt puts it into the British equivalent, indicating that one talent was two hundred and fifty pounds. Goodspeed translates it, "One thousand dollars."

Medical terms should be put into twentieth century, rather than into seventeenth century, idiom. The Greek word which, in Acts 28:8, K.J.V. translates "bloody flux" is really "dysentery." "Palsy" is a corruption of the French *paralysie*, and "paralytic" is a better rendering of a Greek word that literally means "one who has become unstrung." "High fever," rather than "great fever," gives the true sense of Luke 4:38. While "lunatic" or "moon-struck" is the precise equivalent of the Greek word that occurs in Matt. 17:15, modern medical science has abandoned that description of a disease which, from its symptoms, was epilepsy.

Family relationships become clearer when expressed in present-day speech. Mark 1:30, K.J.V., speaks of " Simon's wife's mother." R.S.V. has " Simon's mother-in-law." The word " nephew " has meant a variety of things in the history of our language. It has signified niece, cousin, or " the illegitimate son of an ecclesiastic." In the seventeenth century it often meant grandson or grandchild or lineal descendant. I Tim. 5:4, K.J.V., says, " If any widow have children or nephews." R.S.V. has it: " If a widow has children or grandchildren." In Col. 4:10, Mark is described in K.J.V. as " sister's son to Barnabas "; in R.S.V., as " the cousin of Barnabas."

Barabbas is described in some versions as a " notable " prisoner. The notable people of a community are not ordinarily the ones in jail, and " notorious " seems better to convey the real point. The " upper coasts " of Acts 19:1 refers to a region far from the sea, so that " upper country " is better. One version in Rom. 2:11 says that " there is no respect of persons with God." Young people trained to believe that respect for persons is the foundation of the Christian home as well as of the democratic state find this confusing. The Greek here intends to convey the truth that " God shows no partiality." Some translators have the Pharisees " tempting " Jesus (Mark 10:2). What they were really doing was " testing " him. " Chamberlain of the city " (Rom. 16:23) is a seventeenth century description of the position occupied by Erastus. We should now call him " the city treasurer."

James 1:3 has been translated, " The trying of your faith

worketh patience." "Trying" is used there in the sense of "trying out." To modern ears "trying" sometimes conveys the sense of something irritating or hard to bear. An unruly child tries one's patience and sorrow tries one's faith. The Greek word here, however, has to do with testing. It is used of the testing of metals, by which the genuine is distinguished from the counterfeit. What James has in mind, then, is the assaying of faith, the testing of faith.

Nor does "patience" give an accurate picture of what the author says results from the testing of our faith. The Greek word literally means "a remaining behind." It means "patience" only in the sense of "holding out," "endurance." In the early days of Christian history it was used to describe the virtue shown by martyrs in steadfast endurance, holding out to the very last. What this verse tells us, then, is that "the testing of your faith produces steadfastness."

In this connection it is significant to recall our Lord's word in Luke 21:19 which used to be translated, "In your patience possess ye your souls." It is an injunction used by mothers to overeager children: "Possess your souls in patience." This is a translation that misses the real point. The Greek verb is a commercial term that means "acquire," "purchase," "buy," and here occurs, not as an imperative, but as a simple future. It therefore means "you will buy." It is as if our souls did not belong to us. Steadfast endurance is the price by which we can purchase them. "By your endurance you will gain your lives."

I Peter 2:2 is sometimes rendered, "As newborn babes, desire the sincere milk of the word." This obscures everything. For one thing, it is doubtful whether any housewife will tomorrow leave a note asking the dairyman to leave three quarts of sincere milk. "Sincere" is a term that we now apply to persons rather than to things. How can milk be sincere? The word is evidently used in its original sense (Latin, "without wax"), to translate the Greek word meaning "unadulterated." Those translators best convey the true meaning to twentieth century Americans who make it read "pure milk."

Also, "of the word" misses the true significance. The passage has generally been read as it if were an injunction to take proper quantities of spiritual nourishment, and as a text for emphasizing the importance of Bible study. This is no doubt a desirable thing, but it is not taught in this verse. "Of the word" translates a single Greek word which is the root of our English "logical," and it would be more accurate to render it "the logical and pure milk."

However, it is now known that in New Testament times the word for "logical," "reasonable," or "rational" came to mean "metaphorical," as contrasted with literal. What the author therefore has in mind is pure milk as a symbol of spiritual nourishment. It is urgent that all Christians should be conversant with the Scripture, but at this particular place the author of I Peter is advising his readers to change their spiritual diet: "Put away all malice and all guile and insincerity and envy and all slander," and for that substitute "pure spiritual milk."

Most churchgoers have heard sermons on the text in I Cor. 1:21b, which used to be translated, "It pleased God by the foolishness of preaching to save them that believe." Now preaching as it is practiced by many may very well be a foolish act. One evidence that the Church is a divinely appointed institution is that it has managed to survive nineteen centuries of preaching. But that happens not to be what Paul is talking about in the passage under consideration. The reference in the original is, not to the act of preaching, but to the content of the message, the thing preached.

"It pleased God through the folly of what we preach to save those who believe." Jowett of Balliol said that we were asking a great deal of men to accept as the secret of the universe, as the only key to the meaning of existence, a man who was hanged. That is precisely what Christianity does, although everything depends upon who the man was who was hanged. And that is what Paul is talking about in this particular passage: "the 'sheer folly' of the Christian message." It is only thus that the English New Testament can convey to our eyes and ears what the original Greek conveyed to those who heard and read it first.

৽ 4 ৾

" MANY DIFFERENT LANGUAGES "

Paul wrote to the Corinthians, " There are . . . many different languages in the world, and none is without meaning " (I Cor. 14:10). There speaks a man of culture! The untutored individual has no appreciation of languages other than his own. He thinks the people who use them must be very stupid indeed, and it would be silly for him to exert himself enough to get some appreciation of them. One has heard Americans in Europe shouting English in ever louder tones at taxi drivers, ticket agents, and postal clerks. One woman from a Middle Western state could not read the menu in a Paris restaurant, and the waiter could not understand her request for a sandwich. Walking out in disgust, she exclaimed, " These Frenchmen are so dumb! "

Christians have always been more catholic in their evaluation. The Scriptures were early put into many languages, and one way of finding out what the Bible originally said is to consult the early versions. Translations into Syriac and Egyptian antedate any of our known manuscripts, and Chrysostom in his first homily on Saint John says that the Syrians, Indians, Persians, Ethiopians, and numberless other peoples have translations in their own tongues. When the original text has become corrupt, scholars often find it helpful to consult such an early version and thus find out what the reading was at the time when the translation was made.

Translation has always been an important phase of the missionary's work. Ulfilas, or Wulfila (the " Little Wolf "), appointed by Constantine as fourth century bishop of the Goths, labored for years to convert his adopted countrymen from the worship of Woden and Thor. He translated the Bible into Gothic, and is said to have invented the alphabet that he used. It is interesting that he omitted some of the more warlike portions of the Old Testament. He reasoned that this was the prudent thing to do, since the Goths were already too fond of fighting and " needed in that matter the bit, rather than the spur."

Many suppose that the most important single thing that Martin Luther ever did was to make his German translation of the Bible. He was concerned not only to render the original faithfully but also to render it effectively, so that it would capture the understanding of his fellow citizens. He sometimes spent three or four weeks searching for a single word. When he came to the sacrificial passages of the Old Testament, he went to a meat dealer, who had to kill half a dozen sheep for him and explain the names given to the different parts of the anatomy, so that the translation would be in the living language of the people. He found it difficult to get the Bible authors to speak like Germans, and compared it to trying to teach a nightingale to imitate the cuckoo.

The Reformation was accompanied by translations into many of the languages of Europe. John Calvin was interested in a French version. One of Franklin D. Roosevelt's treasures was the copy of the Dutch Staten Bijbel on which he took the oath of office. This family Bible, with its first entry made in 1693, was in the Nether-German, or Dutch vernacular, a translation made in the first third of the seventeenth century at the behest of the States-General. There was a widespread belief that God had in a special manner presided over the translators. At the time when thousands of Hollanders were dying of the plague, the citizens of Dordrecht, where the scholars did their work, remained untouched by the epidemic.

The first translation into the Turkish language was also made in the seventeenth century by a Pole named Albertus Bobowsky. Kidnaped from his native land by Tartar raiders, Bobowsky was sold as a slave in Turkey. Thereupon he renounced his native faith, embraced Islam, and eventually became dragoman to the sultan. While serving at court, he was persuaded by the Dutch ambassador to undertake a translation of the Christian Scriptures into the Turkish tongue. The work was completed in 1660, and the manuscript sent to Leyden, where it remained unnoticed for one hundred and fifty years. Then a Russian diplomat, Baron von Diez, who had become proficient in the Turkish language while serving as ambassador at Constantinople, discovered it. The British and Foreign Bible Society asked him to edit it for publication, but he died before his revision was complete, and it was not until 1827 that the manuscript was ready for publication. A revision into modern Turkish appeared in 1941. In keeping with the nation's program of modernization, it was printed in Roman characters instead of the formerly used Turkish ones.

The first Bible published in Amharic, the official language of Abyssinia, was issued in 1840. Due to the changing nature of that African tongue, a revision was recently carried out. In 1844 there was first published in Athens a translation of the New Testament into modern Greek. Most of the words are the same as in the original, but there have been changes of grammatical form and structure, and of the shades of words. The term in Eph. 1:14, familiar in English as " earnest," or " guarantee," originally meant " a part given in advance of what will be bestowed fully afterwards." In terms of present-day commercial transactions, " hand money " or " down payment " seems the equivalent. In modern Greek the word, slightly altered in form, has come to mean " engagement ring." New translations are thus ever adding zest to Bible interpretation.

When the Melanesian Mission celebrated its centenary in 1950, there was recalled the martyrdom of J. C. Patterson, first bishop of that region, whose skill as translator did much to establish the various dialects of Melanesia as vehicles of communication. The first Methodist missionary to Korea, Rev. H. G. Appenzeller, who arrived there in 1885, promptly set about translating the Scriptures into the language of the Koreans. Around the turn of the century, the New Testament was translated into Braid Scots, or Broad Scotch, the dialect spoken in the lowlands of Scotland. The Braid Scots version of John 3:7 reads, " Mak nae ferlie o' my words, ' Ye maun be born again! ' "

The first Bible printed on American soil was not in the English language. It was John Eliot's Indian Bible, published in 1663. This was a translation into the language of the Massachusetts Indians. A few copies were printed for distribution in England. These had title pages in English, so that the reader unfamiliar with the Indian tongue could at least know what manner of volume it was. This process has gone on right down to our own time. In the year 1944 there appeared in Spain a fresh translation of the Old and New Testaments, the first ever to have been made in

Spanish from the original languages. It is estimated that, on the average, a version of the Bible in some new language or dialect appears about once a month.

A man who traveled as widely as Paul had plenty of experience with languages other than his own. He had gone on "frequent journeys" and had now and then been in "danger from Gentiles" (II Cor. 11:26). He knew the rigors of travel, and one of these was the difficulty of making oneself understood in strange places. It was no doubt as a result of his own constant itineration that Paul could say, "If I do not know the meaning of the language, I shall be a foreigner to the speaker and the speaker a foreigner to me" (I Cor. 14:11). Instead of the word "foreigner," the King James Version has "barbarian."

Paul evidently had more appreciation than the Greeks did of the worth of languages other than his own. "Barbarian" has come to mean "rude," "savage," "uncivilized." It happens to be a Greek word taken over into English. Its original reference was to people who spoke languages the Greek thought unintelligible. It is, in fact, an imitative word. It describes people who seem to be saying nothing, when they talk, except bar-bar-bar-bar. People like that are *barbaroi*. We do not now believe that people whose tongue we do not understand are necessarily depraved or uncouth, and the word is rightly rendered "foreigner."

He who does not understand a language will discover strange things if he attempts to read it. A student looked up a certain word in a Greek dictionary. The meaning was given as "*ago*," and he was greatly puzzled. He was sure the original was a verb, having to do with carrying out an action, and here it was defined as if it were an adverb meaning "past," "gone by." Then it dawned on him that the dictionary was giving a Latin equivalent. " *Ago* " in Latin means " put in motion," " move," " lead," " drive," " tend," " conduct " —and so the problem was solved. As long as he did not know the language that was being used, he was baffled.

The fact that words mean different things in different languages sometimes produces amusing results. " *Peccavi* " is a Latin term that has made its way into English. It means " I have sinned," and is used as an acknowledgment of transgression. By a play on words, a British general once saved charges on a cablegram. On Feb. 17, 1843, after the surrender of Hyderabad, in the Province of Sind, Sir Charles James Napier wired a one-word message to the British War Office. The word was " *Peccavi*," which the Government officials interpreted correctly. It was not a confession of guilt but meant, instead, " I have Sind."

The composer MacDowell relates that some of his students once sent flowers on his birthday. Inside they put a card with a quotation from *Das Rheingold*. The German words were, " *O singe fort*," meaning, " Oh, sing on." This is an appropriate and graceful thing to say to a musician, but it happened that when MacDowell looked at the card, it was not the German meaning of the words that came to his mind at all, but the French meaning. In French the words mean " O powerful monkey " — not a gracious thing to say to a composer.

The years have not altered the truth of Paul's insight that if we do not know the language that is being used we are foreigners to the speaker, and the speaker a foreigner to us. Stranger yet is it to realize that the same word in the same language may mean different things at different times. Twice in recent years Chaucer has been translated into English! That is to say, the English-speaking men of

Chaucer's time would seem like foreigners to us, and we like foreigners to them. Heraclitus based his philosophy upon the belief that everything is in a constant state of flux. " All things flow," he said. Nowhere can this be more readily established than in the field of language, man's elemental means of communication.

Scientists tell us that one characteristic of living things is their power to grow. " To live is to grow; to grow is to change; to change is to go on creating oneself unendingly." Language belongs to the realm of living things, and is therefore in continual process of alteration and development. Some words take on added stature, some degenerate, none remains static. " Gossip " was once a noble term. It originated as " godship," being used to describe the relation between godparents and godchildren. Apparently there was a good deal of coming and going, leading to trivial and mean conversation, among those thus related. Godship degenerated into gossip.

The magician's favorite term has had a similar unhappy history. " Hocus-pocus " is now flummery, abracadabra, nonsense. It was once a solemn part of the Catholic Mass. *Hoc est corpus* is the Latin phrase for what in English we know as " This is my body." So glibly did the priests recite, " *Hoc est corpus,*" as a prelude to the miracle of transubstantiation that the workers in the black arts took it over as an incantation for any baffling sleight of hand.

" Charis," or " Grace," was used among the Greeks to describe three goddesses who, in their mythology, embodied respectively joy, beauty, and brilliance. Christianity took over the word *charis* and ennobled it. It is the New Testament term for the unmerited favor of God, the outgoing of the divine love, which man can never earn but which God freely bestows. In popular usage it has come to have many secondary meanings. A man delayed on his homeward journey presented a streetcar transfer that, according to the time punched, had expired five minutes before. "That's all right," said the conductor, "you have ten minutes' grace in the use of these." In modern parlance, "Charis" is now the trade name for a commercial product.

A more prosaic illustration of the changing nature of language is to be found in the word "bureau," something we see every day. It was first of all a kind of drugget, or coarse woolen fabric for rugs and the like. Then it came to mean a piece of furniture covered with this material. After that it was used for a piece of furniture used for writing, then for a writing desk with drawers, then for a chest of drawers, then for a room containing this article. After that it was applied to occupations carried on in such a room and to the persons engaged in it, until now it has come to mean a group of persons directing an organization or department, frequently of the Government.

Nowhere is the fascinating story of language changes more readily observed than in the history of the English Bible. In announcing a new edition of the Scripture, a publisher advertised: "Every word of the beloved King James Version intact." If that had been true, few readers would have gone very far in it! In the matter of spelling, for example, the King James Version has undergone a vast amount of modernization. In Matt. 25:20 some editions still have "moe" for "more." Perhaps that is designed for use below Mason and Dixon's line! The original "one iote or one title" (Matt. 5:18) has been changed to "one jot or one tittle" — still difficult enough to understand. The "peny" of Matt. 20:2 has been changed to "penny." "Mint, and annise, and cummine" (Matt. 23:23) are now "mint and anise and cummin" — but who, even yet, is quite sure what those tiny garden vegetables were? Anise is dill; cummin is a dwarf plant of the Near East, long cultivated for its seeds, which are used in flavoring. The " All hayle " of Matt. 28:9 has been changed into the more familiar " All hail " — although Goodspeed thinks we can get its true significance only if we translate it " Good morning! "

Other strange spellings which meet us in older editions of the King James Bible are "fornace " for furnace (Fornax, among the Romans, was the goddess of ovens, whose feast, Fornacalia, was celebrated in February); " charet " for chariot; " murther " for murder; " damosel " for damsel; "fift and sixt" for fifth and sixth; "fet " for fetch; " creeple " for cripple; " moneth " for month. Proper names are even more difficult to recognize, whether of persons or of places. " Osee " is Hosea; " Moyses " is Moses; " Isahac " is Isaac; " Marie " is Mary. In Acts 13:21, Saul is described as the son of Cis.

Place names are probably more confusing than personal ones. " Sina " is Sinai; " Sion " is Zion; " Mileta " is Malta; "Sodoma " is Sodom; " Saron " is Sharon. A present-day edition that should preserve these spellings throughout would merely confuse us, and any edition that does not preserve them is not giving us the original King James.

Not only spelling but also grammar has changed drastically since the seventeenth century. Anyone, for example, who prays, " Our Father who art in heaven " has altered the language of the King James Bible. The latter has it, " Our Father which art in heaven." In the seventeenth century " which " was applied to persons as well as to things. That usage we should now consider quite rude, even as applied to our fellows; it is even more so when applied to the Deity. In this case, the innate sense of the fitness of things has, in most people, already triumphed over bondage to the letter. Rarely does one hear, " Our Father which . . ."

The neuter possessive pronoun " its " does not occur in the King James Bible, as it does not occur in Shakespeare. It is a convenient grammatical form which was not then in use; the masculine possessive pronoun was used in its stead. The King James Bible therefore says, " If the salt have lost his savor." It is quite right that we should now use " its."

One characteristic of present-day versions of Scripture is the abandonment of forms of speech that are no longer in common use. " Whosoever " and " whatsoever " are now simply " whoever " and " whatever." For such phrases as " on this wise " and " set at nought " and for such words as " privily," " wherein," " whereby," " thereabout," and " divers," terms in general use today are substituted. Obsolete terms such as " thou," " thee," " thy," " thine," and the verb endings " est," " edst," " eth," and " th " are replaced by present-day equivalents. The one exception to this is in the prayers of the Bible. Some translators feel that in language addressed to the Deity archaic terms have a certain solemnity which makes it desirable that they be retained.

More than a hundred years ago, in a book written in 1851, Archbishop Trench called attention to the fact that the careful distinction which writers once made between yea and yes, nay and no, had quite disappeared. " Yea " and " Nay " were once the answers to questions framed in the affirmative, as " Will he come? " If the question were posed in the negative, " Will he not come? " the proper answer was either " Yes " or " No." Sir Thomas More found fault with Tyndale that he did not observe this distinction in his translation of the Bible. Matthew 5:37 in the Revised Standard Version translates, " Let what you say be simply

'Yes' or 'No'; anything more than this comes from evil."

Not only have spelling and grammar changed since the seventeenth century, but vocabulary has changed too. Some words still in use have done a complete flip-flop, so that they mean the opposite of what they meant in the seventeenth century. The changing nature of words Dr. Clarence T. Craig illustrated by the little word "drip." Those now in middle years learned when they were in school that that is what comes out of the spigot when the washer is worn. Those in touch with adolescents know that a drip is now something quite otherwise.

A man was scheduled to speak at a college which during its long history had been strictly for girls. The president explained, "Now, however, we have a few co-eds," by which he meant GI's. That seemed strange indeed to one in whose college days all co-eds wore skirts. Thus language lives and grows and changes right before our eyes.

Consider, then, how the religious vocabulary of English-speaking Christians has changed. As reported in the King James Bible, Paul wrote to the Romans (Rom. 1:13), "I purposed to come unto you, (but was let hitherto)." This doesn't seem to make sense. Among us, "let" means "permit," and we should not say, "I purposed to come unto you, *but* was permitted." Actually, of course, "let" in the seventeenth century meant "hinder" or "delay." In the game of tennis, a ball that strikes the top of the net and yet goes on over is a ball that has been hindered in its flight and is called a "let" ball (even though for most players this has been corrupted into "net" ball). The only other survival of this usage is in the notoriously archaic vocabulary of the law, where it occurs in the phrase, "Without let or hindrance."

In I Thess. 4:15, Paul assures his sorrowing friends that

" we which are alive and remain unto the coming of the Lord shall not prevent them which are asleep." The question, an urgent one for the early Christians, had to do with those who had already died: what would befall them in the day of the Lord's return? Paul is sure that the living are not going to " prevent them " — just exactly how does one " prevent " dead people? The answer is that in the King James Version " prevent " is used in its etymological sense of " prae " plus " venio " — that is to say, " come before." What Paul is saying is that the living will not have any advantage over those who have preceded them into the realm of spirits.

In Mark 6:25 the King James Bible tells us that Salome asked for the head of John the Baptist " in a charger " — one wonders exactly what that conveys to the church school student of today. A charger is, among us, a spirited horse; Webster defines it as " an officer's mount for battle or parade." Or is a charger a horse? Isn't it what the garageman uses to rejuvenate our dead battery? In seventeenth century England a charger was " a large flat dish or platter for carrying meat." This makes sense out of the story, though present-day idiom would require us to say " on a platter," rather than " in a platter."

In Acts 12:4 the King James Bible relates that Peter, who had been arrested by Herod Agrippa, was placed in the charge of " four quaternions of soldiers." Anybody who doesn't know what a quaternion is will have to look it up in the dictionary, where he will discover that it is now, first off, a printer's word. A quaternion is a piece of paper that has been folded once and then folded over again, producing a quire. Anyone who cannot quite understand how four pieces of paper folded twice could keep guard over a prisoner will have to read on in the dictionary, where he will discover that a quaternion is " an operator, or factor, Q, multiplication by which converts one vector, A, into another vector, B, by changing the direction and magnitude of vector A so that it agrees with that of vector B." Any who do not yet understand what a quaternion is will be very glad for a present-day-speech version; the Revised Standard has it, " Four squads of soldiers." As a college student put it, " If that's what they meant, why didn't they say it long ago? "

Changes we have been enumerating are such as are wrought by the passing of time. Consider next the vast import of sea changes that have been wrought in our mother tongue. Even Americans are entitled to have the Scripture in a language they can understand. Muriel Lester relates that she was once introduced to an audience in the United States as " a lady from the land across the sea that uses our language." But there are differences, and many a GI discovered that American English is one thing and British English is something else.

It is surprising how great can be the misunderstanding between those who believe themselves to be using the same mother tongue. In Scotland it is a high compliment to a woman to say that she is " homely." It means that she is hospitable and friendly and makes you feel at home. An American woman, on the other hand, would hardly feel complimented upon overhearing someone say he thought her homely. The British statesman does not " run for office," as his American counterpart does; he " stands for election." The British student, on the other hand, does not stand his examinations, as American students do; he sits his examinations.

In connection with the laying of the foundation stone of New College, Edinburgh, on January 3, 1846, the daily paper observed that " the Friends of the undertaking have agreed to Breakfast together in the Saloon of Gibbs' Royal Hotel, Princes Street, on Wednesday morning, at a quarter before Nine o'clock." Subsequent reports indicated that the company that did assemble then " was such, perhaps, as it would be impossible to bring together in any other city or land." American readers are apt to lift their eyebrows at the thought of Scottish theologians assembling in a saloon preparatory to establishing a divinity school.

Actually, Webster lists, " A shop where intoxicating liquors are sold," as the fifth meaning of the word " saloon " and as a usage confined to the United States. The primary meaning of the word, as everyone knows who has ever been on a British ship, is, " A spacious, lofty, and elegant apartment; . . . a large and elaborate drawing room." The Scottish ecclesiastics may or may not have had something to drink before setting out on their pious undertaking, but that cannot be inferred from their place of meeting. The saloon of the Gibbs Royal Hotel was simply a large, elaborately decorated drawing room.

Ignorance of subtle language differences can sometimes cause embarrassment. *Time* magazine reported that the Duchess of Westminster had been " recently divorced." Thereupon the American news weekly received a letter from a firm of British lawyers — called " barristers " over there — demanding a correction. To be divorced, in Britain, implies that a decree has been given against one, and this suggests that one has been the guilty party in whatever wrongs went on. In point of fact, the duchess had been the petitioner, the duke was the guilty party, and the American report brought red faces to all concerned.

Differences between British and American usage caused extensive difficulty during the war when joint operations were under way. Because British and Americans spoke the same tongue, it was assumed that they would always mean the same thing when they used the same word. This proved to be far from the case. When the American troops first arrived in Britain, a request was made to the British War Office for garbage cans. The British replied that they had none, and the Americans promptly requisitioned from home a large supply that would have taken up much valuable shipping space. In the nick of time it was discovered that there was no need after all to ship garbage cans. There were plenty in Britain. The Britishers called them " dustbins."

So marked were the differences in vocabulary that staff officers of both armies had to be given instruction in how the others might be expected to use the mother tongue. The important word " supplies " had different connotations. In British usage it meant simply food, chemicals, etc., consumed on a daily basis. For more permanent materials, such as tools, ammunition, and other heavy goods, the British used the word " stores." What Americans called blowtorches the British called " brazing lamps." Storage batteries were " accumulators," and thumbtacks " drawing pins."

Differences between British and American English have carried over into " peacetime," and have caused difficulties in the United Nations. As if it were not enough that Chinese and Russians and Ethiopians still suffer under Babel's curse, even the Americans and the British do not always understand each other! To table a motion in the United States means to put it aside indefinitely, lay it on the table of the presiding officer, whence it may (but probably will not!) be brought up for future consideration. In

British parliamentary parlance, however, to "table" is to bring up for attention.

Arnold Toynbee confesses that he learned a great historical lesson from a Near Easterner who asked him where he had learned the American language! "We speak it in England too," he said. A bill introduced into the Massachusetts legislature in 1952 would require the removal from all textbooks and commonwealth publications of every reference to the English language, and substitute for it the American language.

The gulf between Americans and Britishers has played its part in Bible publication and translation, even as it increasingly must in the interpretation of the English Bible. At the end of the nineteenth century, separate revisions were issued on the two sides of the Atlantic, the English Revised Version and the American Standard Version. A new official revision is presently being carried out in Britain, authorized jointly by the Church of Scotland and the Church of England.

A striking illustration of the difference between the two languages is to be found in the interpretation of the word "corn." Matthew 12:1 in the King James Version relates that "Jesus went on the sabbath day through the corn; and his disciples were ahungered, and began to pluck the ears of corn, and to eat." In the mind of an American this conjures up a picture of an Iowa cornfield, with ears that have to be plucked and shucked. This gives a false impression, for the Greek words used refer to a grainfield and to the plucking of ears of grain, undoubtedly wheat.

The British reader would not be misled; for, to him, corn is just a general term for grain and is used for the leading cereal crop of a region. In England corn is wheat.

In Scotland corn is oats. In some regions corn could be barley. The Biblical grain was wheat. (The British, not being familiar with Indian corn, can of course be misled in other ways. Scots received from Americans a gift of canned sweet corn, and were wholly baffled by it. They had never seen anything like it and had no idea what to do with it. Since the word " sweet " appeared in the name, and since the Britisher calls his dessert a sweet, they concluded that it must be some strange new way of finishing up a meal!)

An American reader could be further confused if in reading of " a corn of wheat " in John 12:24, he had in mind both maize and wheat. He would think of wheat as one thing and corn as another; and it would seem nonsense to put the two together, until he stopped to think that even in American usage a " corn " is a kernel! A knowledge and appreciation of the varied ways in which words are used serve to increase our sympathies as human beings and help us to understand that there are " many different languages in the world, and none is without meaning."

❧ 5 ❧

"SOME THINGS . . . HARD TO UNDERSTAND"

GRANTED a realization that the Bible was not composed in our tongue, that it has been many times translated, and that we must have it in a language we can understand, it has next to be noted that not even then will the Scripture cease to puzzle. Indeed, there are passages in Scripture that even seem self-contradictory. I John 2:15 says, "Do not love the world or the things in the world," and II Tim. 4:10 relates the sad case of Demas, who, "in love with this present world, has deserted me." Perhaps the best-known verse in the New Testament, however, assures us that "God so loved the world that he gave his only Son" (John 3:16).

The question arises, Why, if God loved the world enough to give his only Son to die for it, must the Christian not love it at all? If love is the supreme Christian virtue, and if being a child of God imposes the obligation of godlike behavior, then it is incomprehensible that we should be commanded not to love that which God supremely loved. The answer partly lies in better translation. In the case of Demas, what the Greek really says is, not that he loved the world, but that he loved "this present age." That is to say, he was a thoroughgoing secularist. That is the clue to the remaining difficulty. The world that in I John we are enjoined not to love is, in the Greek, the same world that in the Johannine Gospel God did love.

As among us, "the world" is used in two different senses. On the one hand, it means life organized apart from God, that philosophy which considers that only things are important — all that we mean by "worldliness." That is paganism — and that "world" the Christian is to shun. On the other hand, as we often sing, "This is my Father's world": it is the creation of his handiwork; it is a thing of wondrous beauty and order; it is the dwelling place of his children; it is the scene of his redeeming act. That world the Christian is to love.

Not all difficulties regarding what seem to be Scriptural contradictions are so easily resolved as that one. To the present-day student of Scripture there is perhaps some satisfaction in the realization that he is not the first to have been puzzled by it. Not even the men of apostolic times always and unfailingly understood each other! II Peter 3:15 f. relates that " our beloved brother Paul wrote to you according to the wisdom given him, speaking of this as he does in all his letters. There are some things in them hard to understand, which the ignorant and unstable twist to their own destruction, even as they do the other scriptures."

If that was the case with men much nearer the source of Christianity than we are, if that situation prevailed on the part of men who had opportunity for mutual counsel and who had the same helpers and fellow workers, how much more may we expect difficulty!

The writer recently had a striking illustration of how confused and confusing people can be when they undertake to interpret the Scripture. Riding on a crowded train, I fell into conversation with a fellow passenger. When she learned that I was especially interested in the study of the New Testament, she exclaimed, "You can help me!" She thereupon unfolded an almost incredible tale of intellectual and spiritual confusion arising out of varied interpretations of the Bible.

To begin with, she was born of a Catholic mother who had died at her birth, and she was baptized into the Roman Catholic Church. Her stepmother was not a Romanist, and the girl grew up as merely a nominal Catholic. From the time she was twelve until she was nineteen she was in the show business as a professional dancer. At nineteen she married and became a Baptist. "I go to my husband's church," she explained, "because I think a wife ought to, but I'm afraid I can never be a good Baptist. The minister is always preaching against dancing and saying that anyone who dances will go to hell. Dancing was once my business; it is now my recreation, and I don't see any harm in it. What do you think?"

"If you were God," said I, "and I danced, would you send me to hell?" "Of course not," she said. "Neither would God," said I. "He would not be less considerate than you, and always the starting point in our thought about him is Jesus. Christianity means that God is like Christ." "I feel like a hypocrite," she continued, "in going and listening to that when I don't believe it." "Your unwillingness to be hypocritical is a very religious quality," I observed; "the bitterest words in the gospel are addressed by Jesus to the hypocrites."

But the conflict regarding dancing was not the only source of her anxiety. "My neighbor," she said, "is a Seventh-Day Adventist, and says I'll go to hell for worshiping on Sunday." "If you were God," said I, "and I worshiped on Sunday, instead of on Saturday, would you send me to hell?'" "No," she said, "certainly not." "Neither would God," said I. "But my neighbor quotes Scripture to prove it." "What Scripture?" "The Fourth Commandment, 'Remember the sabbath day to keep it holy.'" I reminded her that the idea of one day's rest in seven was a Hebrew contribution to the life of mankind, but that the Old Testament itself gives two sanctions for its observance. One is the very anthropomorphic reason that God was wearied with the work of creation and when Saturday came he was ready to knock off for the day. The other is a humanitarian reason: "You shall remember that you were a servant in the land of Egypt . . .; therefore the Lord your God commanded you to keep the sabbath day" (Deut. 5:15). People who had themselves been slaves could appreciate the need for a day off!

I further reminded her that the Christian Sunday does not merely represent a shift of the Jewish Sabbath from one day to another. It is a wholly new and different institution: it commemorates Jesus' rising from the dead, and every Sunday is a "day of resurrection." "But my neighbor says God gave the Ten Commandments and God's law cannot be broken." "But," said I, "for the Christian there are not Ten Commandments but Eleven: 'A new commandment I give to you, that you love one another.' The Ten must always be looked at in the light of the Eleventh. Now, as Augustine said, the Christian law is to 'love God and do what you like.' That means that you and not anybody else or any Church is to be the arbiter for you of right and wrong."

"But my neighbor says very few can be saved — only a certain number." "Could it be 144,000?" I asked. "Yes, that's it. It explains all about it in Revelations [sic]. My stepmother died recently and my neighbor says her soul is sleeping in the grave until the resurrection. Then Christ will come and make up the number of the saved and the rest will burn with fire unquenchable." I then spoke of Jesus' refusal to answer the question, " Will those who are saved be few? " (Luke 13:23). Jesus always insisted that the total number of the saved is not a matter about which the individual need be concerned. His only concern ought to be that he shall be included in the number! I spoke also about the three different words in the Greek Testament, all of which in some versions are translated by the single English term " hell." Only one of them has the idea of fire, and that is a word used of the garbage dump outside Jerusalem.

As if a Roman Catholic mother, a Baptist husband, and a Seventh-Day Adventist neighbor were not enough, this woman's troubles were intensified by a mother-in-law who was a spiritualist. She was sure that communication with the dead was the all-important thing. Her husband, who had died but recently, had promised to summon into the spirit world one who was troubling her. The daughter-in-law was sure this was a thinly veiled reference to herself! To all her other fears and misunderstandings had now been added the threat that she might soon be turned into a ghost!

Mark 5:26 relates the sad case of a woman who had " suffered much under many physicians, . . . and was no better but rather grew worse." This other woman was in an even worse plight. She had suffered many things of many interpreters of Scripture and her understanding was darkened.

How many persons are there in similar case! A wealthy woman, brought up an Episcopalian and married to a Presbyterian, sincerely wanted to find out the way of the

Lord. " One minister tells you one thing," she said, " another minister tells you another. Which are you to believe? "

The Protestant principle, of course, is that each individual has to make up his own mind, upon the basis of all the help that he can get. This means that he must never try to interpret a passage in isolation but must look at it in its setting. This involves not only making sure to quote it straight but also being careful not to wrest it from its Scriptural context. Gordon Poteat (*We Preach Not Ourselves*, page 8, Harper & Brothers, 1944) tells of three ministers, each of whom contended that he used the Scripture properly, always beginning with the question, " What does the Bible say? " " To test themselves they agreed upon a common text for their next sermon. The text chosen was, ' And David danced before the ark.' When they reported on the following Monday it turned out that the first one had proclaimed in his sermon that David danced before there was an ark, but not afterward, and that, therefore, converted folk should not dance. The second sermonized on the agility of David's dancing before the ark and derived the lesson of the need for greater activity in the service of the Lord. The third expounded the text as meaning that there was a sacred enclosure in front of the ark in which David deported himself in a grave ritual dance and taught a lesson in reverent worship. And none of the three realized that he had misquoted the text (II Sam. 6:14): ' And David danced before the Lord with all his might.' "

One has heard prolonged debate on the question whether or not money is the root of all evil. One minister was even known to have accepted a call on the basis of his belief that money was the root of all evil. His former congregation reproached him for making a transfer just because a larger salary was involved. " Well," he explained, " money is the root of all evil. Where the most money is, there the most evil is. Where the most evil is, there the minister most needs to be." The truth is, however, that the Scripture does not say that money is the root of all evil. What it does say is that " the love of money is the root of all evils " (I Tim. 6:10).

Similarly in regard to a saying about truth and freedom: " The truth shall make you free " is a saying often quoted. It is sometimes inscribed on libraries and schoolrooms. While one has never seen it on a science building, there are those who hold that it would be a fitting motto even for a laboratory. It is the slogan and inspiration of many individuals who are engaged in the search for truth. This is not, however, what Jesus said. He made no such unconditional promise. What he did say was, " If you continue in my word, you are truly my disciples, and you will know the truth, and the truth will make you free " (John 8:31 f.). That is to say, Christian discipleship is the route by which one arrives at the truth that sets him free, and there is in the gospel no promise that any other kind of truth has that liberating power.

In one of the Biblical discussions that took place at the court of Charlemagne, the emperor asked Alcuin what hymn it was that Jesus and his disciples had sung together after the Last Supper. The Gospels did not make this clear. Alcuin replied by explaining at length the meaning of the term " hymn," reciting views held by different interpreters as to which hymn this was, and finally stating his own opinion. He was sure it was nothing other than the prayer of Jesus which is recorded in the seventeenth chapter of John.

We are not told whether this explanation satisfied Charlemagne and his courtiers. Familiarity with the life of Bible times would have led to a different answer, and better translation even helps. What the Greek says is, not, "When they had sung a hymn," but simply, "When they had hymned." All trained in Hebrew religious customs would understand at once what was meant. At the Passover meal, which Jesus with his friends was now celebrating — and transforming! — it was customary that the Hallel should be sung. This consisted of Ps. 113 to 118. The first part, Ps. 113 and 114, was sung following the explanation of the significance of the rite by the head of the house, and the second part, Ps. 115 to 118, was sung after the fourth and final cup. In saying, then, that Jesus and his friends "hymned," the writer is plainly telling us that they sang the concluding portion of the Hallel.

Viewing the Scripture in proper perspective involves not only making sure of its Biblical context but also looking at it in its context of time and space. Some things "hard to understand" become clear when seen in the light of their Oriental setting. Jesus was not an Occidental, and his ways of thinking were those native to the Near East, not to the Far West. We can begin to comprehend him only when we try to remove our American-made spectacles and look at him through simpler eyes. When Jesus dispatched the Seventy to go through the villages of Galilee to prepare the way for him, he said to them, "Salute no one on the road" (Luke 10:4). This does not impress us as the way to win friends and influence people. It is particularly difficult to understand how men sent on a mission of good will should be started out with instructions like that.

The answer lies in Oriental custom. Lacking newspapers and radio, the Oriental traveler to this day loves nothing better than to pause in his journey for a long exchange of greetings. His, " Hello! " you will return with, " Two hello's! "; then he says, " Three hello's! " He inquires about your age, your health, and the welfare of all your relatives, even though you and he had not met until that moment. As Jesus himself noted, his contemporaries loved " salutations in the market places " (Luke 11:43; 20:46). For him, time was short; the message of the Kingdom was urgent. That was why his disciples were forbidden to stop for greetings.

Perhaps the sternest word in the gospel is Jesus' saying to a dutiful son, " Leave the dead to bury their own dead " (Luke 9:60). Some find it shocking to think that Jesus would not only encourage but actually command a young man to forget what seems obviously the first of filial responsibilities, the decent interment of his father. We must remember, however, that it was in a semitropical land that Jesus lived, and amid people who had not the modern abomination of desolation, the funeral parlor. The Hebrew did not embalm his dead, and in a hot climate burial had to take place immediately. It seems likely, therefore, that this man's father had not yet died, else the son even now would have been attending to the last rites. What he was really saying was: " Wait until our family matters are all straightened out; wait until my father dies and I receive my share of the inheritance; then I will come and follow you." Jesus cannot abide such cool and calculating delay and solemnly says, " Leave the dead to bury their own dead; but as for you, go and proclaim the kingdom of God."

A stern word that has troubled many is Jesus' warning to those who trust in riches: " It is easier for a camel to go through the eye of a needle than for a rich man to enter the kingdom of God " (Mark 10:25; cf. Matt. 19:24; Luke 18:25). In the walls that surround Oriental cities there are gates that can be opened wide, and within these are smaller gates for pedestrians. Through one of these latter, a camel, if stripped of his load, might be able to squeeze, and so this passage has by many been held to refer to the postern gate. The difficulty is that in the ancient world the postern gate was never referred to as " the eye of a needle." In so far as that title is now applied, it seems to have arisen from the Westerner's attempt to tone down this saying.

In the hope of modifying the saying, the text has become corrupt. Some minor manuscripts change the Greek *theta* to *iota*. That slight alteration, comparable to that from *e* to *i* in English, shifts the meaning from " camel " to " cable," the kind of rope that might be used to hold an anchor or fasten a boat to shore. Even so, to get such a rope through a needle's eye is still an impossibility. Jesus no doubt intended to state an impossibility. The Kingdom is not open to those who trust in wealth; it requires humility and sacrifice. This vivid contrast between the largest beast of burden and the smallest of man-made openings is in accord with Jesus' use of the absurd.

This kind of contrast would be readily understood by the Oriental. A rabbi who did mighty deeds was known as a mover of mountains, and so Jesus says (Matt. 21:21), " If you have faith and . . . say to this mountain, ' Be taken up and cast into the sea,' it will be done." He pictures the hypocrites, concerned only with the trivia of the law, as " blind guides, straining out a gnat and swallowing a camel! " (Matt. 23:24). The Oriental was fond of gestures which expressed his emotions better than words, and so Jesus bids his disciples, if they do not receive a friendly welcome in any community, to " shake off the dust from your feet as a testimony against them " (Luke 9:5).

A passage of Scripture must be looked at in its setting.

Another principle of the Reformers was — and of the Reformed Churches is — that when any passage of Scripture is difficult to understand, the interpreter must consider it also in the light of other passages bearing on the same subject. John Wesley said, " I search after and consider parallel passages of Scripture, comparing spiritual things with spiritual." This principle is explicitly stated in the Westminster Confession of Faith: " The infallible rule of interpretation of Scripture is the Scripture itself; and therefore, when there is a question about the true and full sense of any Scripture (which is not manifold, but one), it may be searched and known by other places that speak more clearly " (Chapter I, section 9).

Not all groups realize this, and some build a whole theology upon isolated phrases occurring in a single translation. In the long-suppressed preface to the King James Bible the translators ask: " Is the Kingdom of God become words or syllables? Why should we be in bondage to them if we may be free? " There are sects for whom the Kingdom of God is words and syllables. They sometimes fashion an entire system out of a particular translation of a single word. The so-called " Holiness " Churches were extremely unhappy with the first printing of the Revised Standard New Testament.

They felt that the very ground on which they stood had been cut from under them. Their distinctive word had been exscinded from what they considered crucial passages. They were sure that the Greek word *hagiazo* meant " sanctify," while the Revised Standard translators generally rendered it " consecrate." A part of our Lord's high-priestly prayer was made to read: " Consecrate them in the truth. . . . For their sake I consecrate myself, that they also may be consecrated in truth " (John 17:17, 19).

The root idea seems to be "set apart." When Moses bade the people sanctify themselves (e.g., Ex. 19:10), he was not urging them to obtain the second blessing, but rather to make of themselves a people separated unto God.

The Holiness groups felt further offended by a change in Acts 19:2. Even if the word "sanctify" was gone, they could still insist that their belief in the second blessing was substantiated by that passage which the King James renders, "Have ye received the Holy Ghost since ye believed?" Here plainly, they said, is the Biblical ground of their theology. The persons thus addressed had been converted. Subsequent to that — "since ye believed" — they had become eligible for a second blessing. This cannot be substantiated by the Greek, where both verbs are in the same tense, one being a participle to express action contemporaneous with that of the main verb. The Revised Standard Version renders it, "Did you receive the Holy Spirit when you believed?"

So also with "dispensationalism." The favorite word of this group occurs but four times even in the King James Version. The Revised Standard has eliminated it entirely, replacing it by "commission" in I Cor. 9:17; "plan" in Eph. 1:10; "stewardship" in Eph. 3:2; and "divine office" in Col. 1:25. Thus the special word upon which this system depends is missing, and once again there is illustrated the danger of basing great doctrines on isolated passages or precarious renderings.

The makers of the Revised Standard Version were wholly unaware that they were omitting anybody's favorite theological terms. Working to give English readers the best possible rendering of the Greek, they chanced to pass over words dear to the hearts of some. When the whole Bible appeared in the Revised Standard Version, "sanctify" had been restored in some passages. Any group, however, is in a desperate case if its principal doctrine is found to rest upon words and syllables.

Scripture must always be judged by Scripture. A true doctrine of Christian tolerance, for example, can be established only thus. Jesus says at one time, " He that is not against us is for us " (Mark 9:40), implying that a certain gracious inclusiveness ought to characterize Christ's followers. Anyone not bent on doing them harm may safely be put down as being on their side. On the other hand, Jesus also said, " He who is not with me is against me " (Luke 11:23). This would seem to suggest rigid exclusiveness: only those are on our side who call themselves by our name, accept our presuppositions, follow our techniques.

A man could build up a system on either of these sayings: the liberal on the one, the obscurantist on the other. Actually, both must be taken into account. There are times when the Christian movement may claim as having on its side all who are not in active opposition. The scientist with his love of truth may not acknowledge himself to be religious, but in so far as he is devoted to the selfless pursuit of truth, that is being religious — and the Church ought to recognize in him an ally. On the other hand, there are times of moral crisis and danger when indecision and indifference may imperil the truth — in which case, anybody not willing to stand up and be counted has to be listed with the opposition.

So with the Scriptural doctrine regarding the State. Paul and Peter are agreed that the Christian must be in subjection to constituted authority (I Peter 2:11-25; Rom. 13:1-7). In Lutheranism this has been interpreted to mean that the Church is to have nothing whatever to say about the affairs of the State — these are to be left entirely in the hands of kings and governors. These particular passages, however, have to be compared with other Biblical teaching on the subject. It is true that man must render unto Caesar the things that belong to Caesar (Matt. 22:21), but it is equally true that he must render unto God the things that belong to God.

By precept and example the Scripture makes it plain that lordship of conscience does not belong to the State, and any claim by the civil power to primacy at this point must be rejected by the Christian. Also, the teaching of both Paul and Peter on this score has to be interpreted in the light of what those worthies did in times of conflict. When Peter was forbidden by the magistrates to preach in the name of Christ (Acts 5:28 f.), he paid no attention whatever, except to assert, "We must obey God rather than men." In a number of cities Paul refused to obey "cease and desist" orders from the local government, and willingly endured stonings, scourgings, and imprisonment rather than be silent about a Christ of whose lordship the Romans were afraid.

In I Cor. 7:1 Paul says, "It is well for a man not to touch a woman," and in v. 26 he urges the unmarried to remain as they are. This chapter has been used to justify celibacy. Commenting on it, Origen stresses that the apostle uses the Greek word *kalon*, meaning "good," or "beautiful," of celibacy, whereas all that he says of marriage is that it is not sin. Taken by itself, the passage might seem to indicate an absolute conviction that it is better to be unmarried than married.

Scripture, however, must be interpreted by Scripture, and several points must here be noted. First, this passage does not pretend to be a complete treatise on marriage. It was written in answer to a question asked by the Corinthians. This is apparent from the introduction, " Now concerning the matters about which you wrote " (I Cor. 7:1); but we do not know what the specific question was. If we were thoroughly acquainted with the question, we could no doubt understand the answer better, and a different question might have elicited a different answer.

In the second place, this was an answer to a question that had been asked by Corinthian Christians. Corinth was noted for its licentiousness and immorality. Sexual irregularity was even joined with pagan worship. Its Temple of Aphrodite had a thousand sacred prostitutes. If we fully understood conditions faced by the Christian community in that kind of environment, we should be better able to comprehend the nature of the apostle's answer to their question. In any case, this was a word addressed to the Corinthians and does not appear to be a universal dictum.

In the third place, the question was asked and the reply given at a time of great external stress. Paul's response is given " in view of the impending distress " (I Cor. 7:26). The exact nature of that distress also is unknown to us. Some think it the famine mentioned in Acts 11:28, a famine known to have been long and severe, particularly in Greece. (Cf. J. A. Bengel, *Gnomon of the New Testament, in loc.* T. & T. Clark, 1886.) If that were the unpleasant situation Paul had in mind, it would be understandable why he would advise people not to complicate the situation by marriage and the bringing of additional stomachs into the world.

It seems more likely, however, that the distress had to do with the expected end of the age and the " woes of the Messiah " spoken of in the apocalyptic literature. The birth pangs of the new era would involve everyone in tension and uncertainty, and in that situation it did not seem wise for one to contract marital obligations. If the time were short, as Paul seems to have expected, then one's external state was a matter of no great concern. This is suggested by what Paul says elsewhere in the chapter: in view of the impending end, even slavery is not galling.

Finally, what Paul here says about the advantages of celibacy has to be set off, not only against what he himself elsewhere says, but against the whole tenor of Biblical thought on the subject. The Hebrews never viewed marriage in any other light than that it was completely normal and desirable. The ascetic tendency, early introduced into the Christian Church, represented a Greek view of the flesh, not the Hebrew view. Marriage was not only honorable, but it was a duty, and Ps. 127 celebrates the result of marriage:

> " Lo, sons are a heritage from the Lord,
>   the fruit of the womb a reward.
> Like arrows in the hand of a warrior
>   are the sons of one's youth.
> Happy is the man who has
>   his quiver full of them!
> He shall not be put to shame
>   when he speaks with his enemies
>   in the gate " (Ps. 127:3-5).

Paul prided himself upon being a Hebrew of the Hebrews, and it is difficult to think of him as repudiating this elementary concept of Israel. It is further to be noted that in the Ephesian letter Paul uses marriage as a symbol of the relationship between Christ and his Church: " Husbands, love your wives, as Christ loved the church and gave himself up for her " (Eph. 5:25). For Paul there could be nothing in heaven or earth more sacred than the relationship between Christ and his bride, the Church. The man who could use figures of speech like that evidently did not take a low view of marriage!

The Scripture seems to have a contradictory attitude on burden-bearing. One of the most frequently quoted injunctions of Christian morality is, " Bear one another's burdens, and so fulfil the law of Christ " (Gal. 6:2). Not so well known is a saying of the same author in the same context: " Each man will have to bear his own load " (Gal. 6:5). Is our principal obligation, then, to bear the load for other people or to carry our own burdens? Plainly the two commands must be weighed off the one against the other.

There have been men devoted to great causes who were so concerned with lightening the load of others that they did not bear their own burden, and so added to the load others were having to shoulder. Doers of good are particularly subject to this misguided endeavor. A husband and father travels extensively for a noble enterprise. " We have almost no home life," his wife complains " — or at least he doesn't. I have plenty." The husband had been widely praised for bearing other people's burdens, but was neglecting a prior obligation to carry his own part of the domestic load. Perhaps he is the one who should have heeded Paul's advice to the Corinthians about celibacy.

There are wives who put the needs of anyone else ahead of the requirements of their own family. On the slightest excuse they will pick up and go somewhere to comfort a friend or assist a cause or play bridge, leaving their own children to fend for themselves. In the King James translation of the two passages cited above, " burden " is used in each. There are two different Greek words, however. " His own load " which a man has to bear is represented by the

Greek term for a soldier's pack. He cannot expect anybody else to carry that for him, and bearing it for himself is prior to anything else he can do. The "burdens" of others that we are to bear are loads of grief and anxiety and responsibility which we voluntarily share.

✑ 6 ☙

"YOU SEARCH THE SCRIPTURES"

THE CHOIR in a certain church was severely criticized for using an anthem which, the critics held, was susceptible of a double meaning. The anthem was based on the last two verses of Ps. 139. The passage begins, " Search me, O God," and has reference to the divine scrutiny of our hidden selves. The objection was to the use of that anthem as an offertory! It was pointed out that the " Search me, O God " had implications not intended at the time of the collection. To search does mean to " go through and examine for the purpose of finding or ascertaining something." Children know that when the sheriff arrests a man, the first thing he does is to search him, not simply in quest of his loot but also to remove all dangerous weapons in his possession.

These same children are early taught that it is their duty to " search the Scriptures," although the object of the quest is usually not made plain. The authority for this injunction is the King James rendering of John 5:39 f.: " Search the Scriptures; for in them ye think that ye have eternal life: and they are they which testify of me. And ye will not come to me, that ye might have life." On the face of it this does not seem to make sense. On the one hand, Jesus is bidding the people search the Scriptures;

on the other he is assuring them that he only is the source of life.

The difficulty arises out of the fact that the Greek verb in the form in which it appears here can be either indicative or imperative. The King James translators chose to make it imperative, thus robbing it of any meaning. Obviously it is in the indicative mood. Jesus is not exhorting the Jews; rather is he contrasting the practice of looking for salvation in a book with the Christian doctrine that one ought to look for it in a Person: "You search the scriptures, because you think that in them you have eternal life; and it is they that bear witness to me; yet you refuse to come to me that you may have life." Diligent study of the Scripture may be useful, but it is not here enjoined. Here, instead, it is contrasted with the true religion which finds its fulfillment in a Person rather than in a book.

These words are represented by the Fourth Evangelist as having been spoken at "a feast of the Jews." Nobody can be sure quite what feast. Some consider it to have been Pentecost; others, the Passover. The Fourth Gospel is full of chronological perplexities, and some consider the Feast of Purim to involve the smallest difficulty here. In any case, a feast was a time when special attention was called to the Scripture. There were public readings from it, and, in the case of Purim, a dramatization of parts of the story of the deliverance of the Jews from Haman. It would be quite in keeping with Jesus' usually pointed utterances for him to choose such a time to contrast the lifeless religion of book-searching with the life abundant brought by himself. Religion no longer consists in "learned trifling."

This is a lesson in the use of Scripture that has been hard for the Church to learn. One has heard of the woman who said she had always thought the Bible was "just a book to look up texts in," and there are some who think that skill at doing that constitutes religious excellence. A teacher in the junior department of a church school considers her job well done when her pupils have memorized the books of the Bible in order. A junior church organization conducted contests to see who could find references most quickly, and the first one to find it was to read it. As exercises in familiarizing young people with the location of different parts of the Bible, such procedures may be useful, but youngsters can become quite proficient at it without capturing anything at all of the spirit of the Bible, and some who could recite the list backward had no idea what a prophet was or what any prophet stood for. And, after all, there is a table of contents printed in the front of every Bible!

Searching the Scriptures has sometimes been carried out in organized and grandiose fashion. The Assembly of God, a Pentecostal Church of Covington, Indiana, ushered in the year 1948 with a Bible marathon. The reading of the Scripture began on New Year's Eve, with 160 readers assembled in the Fountain County Courthouse. New Year's Day was Thursday, and it was expected that the reading of the entire Bible would be completed by 8 A.M. Sunday; the readers were expected to average 15 chapters per hour. A public-address system carried the reading throughout the town square. A sleet storm interrupted the community's electrical supply for a time early Thursday, but the reading continued by oil lamp.

Subsequent reports in the public press indicated that the reading was actually completed ahead of time, the end having been reached at 2:21 A.M. Sunday — 74 hours and 21 minutes after its start at midnight on New Year's Eve. The final tally showed that 176 persons had participated in the project, reading in 30-minute shifts. Nearly half of the town's 2,100 inhabitants were reported to have been present for some part of the reading, and approximately 100 were on hand at the conclusion. These all pledged themselves " to read at least one chapter of the Bible during 1948."

Rev. B. B. Minton, pastor of the congregation that sponsored the reading, said that he had noticed " a marked effect " on the morals of the community. No case of juvenile delinquency was reported while the reading was under way, and a policeman stated that he had never seen the courthouse square so " quiet and orderly." He believed that other communities ought to have similar readings, and that " if the United Nations representatives would have begun their sessions with readings from the Bible, divine Providence would have intervened and the sessions would not have broken up in discord."

The Covington achievement does not appear to have established a record so far as time is concerned. The Pentecostal Church of God in Baltimore claimed the world championship nonstop Bible-reading record. Starting one Saturday night, Rev. John William Pitcher and his flock read in relays until they completed the Bible. Their time was 52 hours and 25 minutes. As if Bibles for searching were not already plentiful, a South Dakota newspaper published the whole of the Scripture in installments, running it as a serial. Publication in this fashion required 22 years. The first chapters were published in 1907, and subsequent sections ran continuously until 1929.

Some perhaps ought to search the Scripture more than they do, since they seem to regard it with superstitious awe and assume it to contain what it does not. Hollywood, for example, does not seem yet to have discovered that the marriage ceremony is not in the Bible, as moving-picture clergymen invariably appear to be reading it from that volume, in which, of course, it never was published. *Parade*, a weekly magazine that was formerly circulated with Saturday editions of certain daily papers, once ran a quiz that reflected this influence. One of the questions was, "How many wives does the Bible allow for each man?" The answer was: "Sixteen (four better, four worse, four richer, four poorer)."

In the autumn of 1948 the ecclesiastical member of the Film Censorship Board in Spain succeeded in having the motion picture *Gentleman's Agreement* banned from that land, on the ground that it contained half a dozen "theological errors," one of which was that the Christian obligation to cultivate love and good will extended even to Jews. Members of the Roman Catholic hierarchy in the United States indicated that that was not the official position of the Roman Church. Eric Johnston, representing the Hollywood interests, forthwith set out for Spain and persuaded Franco to lift the ban. Johnston reported that he had told Franco, a good Roman Catholic, that "Love thy neighbor" is one of the Ten Commandments. When a British newsman asked which of the ten, Johnston declared that he would discuss movie problems, but not religious ones. (The controversy is reported in *The New York Times*, September 30 and October 1, 1948; *Time* magazine, October 25, 1948.)

Concerning a new translation of the New Testament, a woman asked: "What does it do to the fundamentals? What does it do to the Ten Commandments and the Apostles' Creed?" This woman was not on the fringe of the congregation, but was a leading worker in the church school and in the women's association.

There is no doubt that a merely verbal knowledge of Scripture may sometimes prove useful in unexpected ways. For example, it has sometimes enabled military men to circumvent wartime censorship. Rev. M. E. Aubrey, General Secretary of the Baptist Union, told the annual assembly of that body of a chaplain who wrote home that he could not give his whereabouts but quoted the remark of one of his men: " Padre, I reckon Abraham was a wise guy to get out of this place as soon as he could, even if he didn't know where he was going." Aubrey said this was passed by the censor, who obviously did not recall the passages in Genesis and Hebrews which relate how " Abraham . . . went out, not knowing where he was to go " (Heb. 11:8).

In his address before the General Assembly of the Church of Scotland, a British admiral related how, early in World War II, his Bible helped him to get a convoy through to Russia: " We were hammered pretty badly for two days from the air, so much so that I was getting very, very worried," he said. " I was turning over in my mind whether I should go on and risk the losses or turn back for home. There was a lull. I took out my Bible and opened it, quite indiscriminately. I read, ' When thou passest through the waters, I will be with thee; . . . when thou walkest through the fire, thou shalt not be burned.' I said to my chief of staff: ' It's all right. We are going through and we shall not lose another ship! ' And we didn't " (*The New York Times,* June 26, 1948).

There is nobody, however, who will suppose that either of these instances represents the Scriptural use of Scripture. The Scripture is given to lead us to Christ, not to help us to avoid the irksome restrictions of wartime censorship, nor yet to offer encouragement to men bent on missions of destruction.

The rabbis of our Lord's time were accustomed to search the Scripture. They were called Sopherim, a word meaning either " those occupied with books " or " those who count." They counted each word and letter of the Scripture. They were to pass on everything exactly as they had received it. It is said of the great rabbi Hillel that he was accustomed to mispronounce a word because his teacher had done so. He knew that it was wrong, but the scribe was to be like " a well-plastered cistern that loses not a drop." The effort was to pass on the law precisely as it had been received, and at the same time apply it to new situations as they arose. It was held that a scribe was to be believed if he said right was left, and one exciting subject of debate was whether it was lawful to eat an egg that had been laid on the Sabbath.

So important were the decisions of the rabbis that it was believed that their judgments were of greater import than the Scripture itself. These men examined the sacred writings minutely, sought for hidden meanings, and uttered their comments authoritatively. These were the men of whom our Lord elsewhere said, " For the sake of your tradition, you have made void the word of God " (Matt. 15:6; cf. Mark 7:13).

Perhaps the basic cleavage between Jesus and the Pharisees was over the question of nationalistic hopes and aspirations. Yet a part of it also had to do with the literal interpretation of the Scripture, except that in the case of the Pharisees it was often the interpretation itself that was the object of veneration. They regarded it as a greater wrong to teach what was contrary to the precepts of the scribes than what was contrary to the Torah itself. It is no wonder that Jesus reproached them for slavish devotion to a book which obscured for them the life-giving power of a Person.

The business of counting words and letters can be put to unexpected uses. The Baconians have found Bacon's signature cryptically inserted in the works of Shakespeare, and thus they arrive at the conclusion that the works attributed to Shakespeare could not have been written by the bard of Avon. It is an interesting fact, however, that if one looks at the Forty-sixth Psalm he will find, in the King James Version, that the forty-sixth word is " shake." If he starts from the end and counts backward, the forty-sixth word is " spear." It is not clear, however, what this proves: whether that Bacon didn't write Shakespeare or that Shakespeare did write the Forty-sixth Psalm!

A good deal of Biblical teaching in our time is on no higher level. Men and women continue to " search the scriptures," counting the verses, the words, the letters. Some who have not heard the term " cabala " suppose that there is deep spiritual significance in the arrangement of such terms. The Pittsburgh *Sun-Telegraph* for June 1, 1947, stated, in answer to the question, " How many chapters, verses, and words are there in the Bible? ": " According to one count, the St. [*sic!*] James version of the Bible has 1,189 chapters; 31,173 verses; 773,692 words; it contains a total of 3,566,480 letters, and the word ' and ' appears in the Bible 46,227 times."

A Bible produced by the Gideons is prefaced with a " Synopsis of the Books of the Bible," with analysis of the various sections, the whole concluding with a statistical analysis listing the number of chapters, verses, and words for each book. This reminds us, however, more of Mohammedanism than of Christianity. The Muslim knows that his Koran has 6,239 verses, 77,934 words, 323,621 letters (P. K. Hitti, *The Arabs,* page 35. Princeton University Press, 1944).

Aside from the fact that all such statistics are hopelessly alien to the spirit of Christianity, a little thought will suggest that counting the words can only be a meaningless exercise in logomachy. Which translation has that many words? And if, as all Protestant Churches recognize, it is the original languages of Scripture that are authoritative, what can possibly be the point in counting the *English* words? It sometimes requires several English words to translate a single Greek term. In Heb. 8:5 the " was admonished of God " of the King James Version is in the Greek a single word. Derived from the Greek noun for " thing," this term originally meant " carry on business, have dealings, negotiate "; it came to be applied to those consulting an oracle, and ultimately signified " give a divine command or admonition." The form here is in the passive voice; the " of God " is not expressed at all, but only implied in the verb. How many words, then, shall we count here — four or one? It would take only a few such passages to make nonsense out of the enumeration of the words.

The chapter and verse reckoning, as will presently be shown, is not in much better case. Passing over for the moment the fact that it is the King James and not the St. James Version (James, " God's silly vassal," was very far from being a saint!), we may even ask, " *Whose* King James Bible contains that many words, etc.? " That is to say, the original King James Bible, still in use in some churches, contained the Apocrypha and therefore had *more* books, chapters, verses, words, letters than the King James Bible now commonly obtainable.

A college course in Bible was based on The Gospel According to Matthew. The principal requirement so far as the students were concerned was the memorization of a " key " verse for each chapter, so that if the teacher quoted the verse the student could identify the chapter and if the teacher mentioned a chapter the student could recite the verse. One has heard a leader at a national religious assembly relate what he thought was the total number of verses in the Bible, and add, " Every one of them has a key word." The " key verse " and " key word " theory is a form of cabalism based on a fundamental misconception of the nature of the Biblical material. The Biblical authors had no thought of inserting key verses in chapters, because they didn't write in chapters. They had no thought of putting key words in verses, because they didn't know anything about verses. Both chapter and verse divisions are a comparatively modern addition to the Scripture.

It might, indeed, be contended that one of the finest insights the student can get into the study of the Scripture is to forget the chapter divisions. The thirteenth chapter of I Corinthians is familiar: from childhood we have delighted in Paul's picture of what love is and does. We miss half its point, however, by detaching it from what goes before and what comes after. What we call ch. 12 (Paul didn't call it that: he was writing a letter and letters don't have chapters) deals with various gifts that men esteem in the church: teaching, healing, administration, etc. These all are valued and valuable, but Paul hastens to add: " And I will show you a still more excellent way " — whereupon he describes the gift of love, without which all else is worth nothing. What we know as ch. 14 begins with the insistence that this love which he has been talking about is to be set before us as life's goal: " Make love your aim."

We are familiar with the picture in the tenth chapter of John of Jesus as the Good Shepherd. Much, however, of its true significance we miss by not reading it continuously with ch. 9, from which the author never dreamed that it would be detached. Chapter 9 pictures Jesus' encounter with the man born blind, and what the religious leaders of the time did to him for allowing himself to be healed on the Sabbath: " they cast him out " (John 9:34). They who were supposedly the guardians of the flock, they who should have been the first to discern the spiritual values that were at stake, proved themselves false and faithless shepherds. By contrast consider what Jesus did: he not only healed the man, but afterward sought him out with a further message. How much more meaning, then, attaches to the saying: " I am the good shepherd. The good shepherd lays down his life for the sheep. He who is a hireling and not a shepherd, whose own the sheep are not, sees the wolf coming and leaves the sheep and flees. . . . He flees because he is a hireling and cares nothing for the sheep " (John 10:11 ff.).

Many a stewardship sermon has been preached from Paul's words in I Cor. 16:1: " Now concerning the contribution for the saints." But this gains untold significance when read as a continuation of ch. 15, where Paul has been talking in exalted terms of the resurrection and its meaning. He made no break between ch. 15 and ch. 16, and saw nothing incongruous in saying: " Thanks be to God, who gives us the victory. . . . Now concerning the contribution." In the Scottish Church the offering is presented at the close of service as the climax of the act of worship. Here in Paul's impassioned correspondence the obligation to support the needy is joined to the cosmic fact of the resurrection, and "what . . . God has joined together, let no man put asunder."

The chapter division between Luke, chs. 6 and 7, is misleading. Luke 7:1, in Luke's manner (cf. chs. 4:30, 37, 44; 5:11, 16, 26; 6:11), is obviously the conclusion of what has gone before and not the introduction to what follows. So also John 5:1 properly belongs to John, ch. 4. On Luke, chs. 17 and 18, Weymouth comments: "The division of chapters at this point is somewhat unfortunate. The reference in v. 8 to the Coming of the Son of Man shows that there is a close connexion between chs. 17:20-37 and 18:1-8" (*The New Testament in Modern Speech,* page 212, note 7. James Clarke & Co., London, 1916).

The division between Acts, chs. 21 and 22, could be ludicrous. The concluding verse of Acts, ch. 21, is as follows: "And when he had given him leave, Paul, standing on the steps, motioned with his hand to the people; and when there was a great hush, he spoke to them in the Hebrew language, saying" — that's the end: what he says is in the next chapter. It has been suggested that the Scripture reading in church some Sunday might conclude thus: "'And when there was a great hush, he spoke to them in the Hebrew language, saying' — here endeth the reading of the lesson."

We cannot understand the Scripture without ignoring chapter and verse divisions. Mathematics has nothing to do with the life of the spirit. The Scriptures do bear witness to Christ, but he himself is the life-giver: "You search the scriptures, because you think that in them you have eternal life; and it is they that bear witness to me; yet you refuse to come to me that you may have life." The Fourth

Gospel represents Jesus' ministry as being almost wholly in terms of life. The prologue says, " In him was life, and the life was the light of men." Scientific thought has shown an intimate connection between life and light. In the world of nature, life is sustained by the process of photosynthesis, and the relation between light and energy is still under investigation. Jesus was not talking about the physical world, but it may yet turn out that that world is governed by the same laws as what those trained in the Greek tradition think of as the spiritual world: life and light may be the same.

Jesus is reported to have said, " I came that they may have life, and have it abundantly " (John 10:10). Jesus thus contrasts himself with other teachers: " All who came before me are thieves and robbers " (John 10:8). This is a hard saying. Can it refer to Amos and Hosea and Isaiah and Jeremiah? Hardly, because Jesus was profoundly influenced by those in Israel's prophetic tradition, and it is impossible to think of him as dismissing that noble company in such ignoble terms. Clement of Alexandria thought that Jesus was thus referring to the Greek philosophers. Philo held that whatever was true in the Greek philosophies was stolen from Moses, and the early Christians, following Jewish precedent, contended that the Greeks stole their wisdom from the Old Testament, even as Prometheus stole the divine fire.

Apparently what Jesus really meant shines out only by way of contrast. That is to say, other teachers, who did not set out to injure or to destroy, fell short of the completeness of truth, and in so doing wasted life and the substance of life. The difference between Jesus and the Old Testament worthies comes out in a comparison of the use of miraculous power attributed to them. Jesus' miracles are life-bringing and life-sustaining, while many Old Testament miracles are life-restricting and even life-destroying.

Take the matter of that loathsome disease, leprosy. In the Old Testament, God's power is manifest by inflicting leprosy upon people. When Miriam protests the marriage of Moses with a Cushite woman, she is smitten with leprosy "as white as snow" (Num. 12:10). When King Hezekiah usurped the priest's functions and ventured to offer incense upon the altar, "leprosy broke out on his forehead" (II Chron. 26:19). Our Lord, however, never inflicts leprosy upon anybody. Instead, he cures leprosy, and not only heals but places his hand upon the leper in token of fellowship restored.

Other incidents, too, highlight the contrast. When Jeroboam touched the altar, his hand was dried up and withered (I Kings 13:4). Jesus never withers anybody's hand; instead, he heals the man with the withered hand (Mark 3:1 ff.). In the Old Testament, the earth opens and swallows people (Num. 26:10); Jesus calls an entombed man from the earth (John 11:43 f.). In the Old Testament, cattle and populace are afflicted with sudden death. In the Gospels, Jesus not only restores people to life but feeds the multitude. Never in his relations with people does Jesus use his great power destructively! He came that people might have life.

The Fourth Evangelist tells us that "Jesus the Life Bringer" was the theme of his Gospel: "Jesus did many other signs in the presence of the disciples, which are not written in this book; but these are written that you may believe that Jesus is the Christ, the Son of God, and that believing you may have life in his name" (John 20:30 f.). Those who companied with our Lord in the days of his flesh did not believe merely that he had introduced a new religion or a new form of an old religion, nor yet that he could be compassed in the pages of a book, but that in him men had, for the first time, been confronted with *life*.

This life was obtained through believing on his name. Among the people of Bible times, the name stood for the whole personality. Men tried to keep their name from the enemy, lest he destroy them. Until Christ came, God's name was so sacred that men dared not pronounce it, but in Christ, God's name was fully made known, and was found to be Love. A Hindu when first confronted by the gospel said, " All my life I have known Him, and now you have told me His name."

This life is a present possession, not merely a future hope. Men ordinarily assume that life comes first, then death, and after that, if they have been good, eternal life. But the New Testament inverts the natural order: " We know that we have passed out of death into life, because we love the brethren " (I John 3:14). Our normal state is a state of death: it is not until our life is hid with Christ in God that we have really begun to live. Relationships that cannot be carried out in his name are already dragging us down to death, and those whose hearts are filled with hatred are already in torment, actually worse off than if they were merely dead.

The time has come when the Christian Church must proclaim boldly that it is in Christ himself — and not merely in books about him — that life is to be had, and that this is the only life worth living. Science in recent decades has had as one of its major aims the extension of man's physical life. In spite of all that war has been doing to obliterate human life, it was assumed that the lengthening of the mortal span would be a universal boon. One such scientist received quite a shock. At a meeting of the

National Academy of Science held, between the wars, in Cleveland, Dr. Wilder Bancroft, professor of chemistry at Cornell, announced that he was on the trail of a method that would increase the number of man's days.

With a proud smile the professor reported that small doses of sodium rhodanate would prolong life at least two years beyond its present span. Expecting to be hailed as a public benefactor, Dr. Bancroft was astonished at the chilly reception that greeted his announcement. Some of his colleagues appeared to regard him as a public enemy, considering that it would be cruel further to stretch human beings upon the rack of torture provided by those times. That may very well be a proper indictment if life is thought of merely in physical terms. In Christ there is life that is life indeed. Pleasures are purer and home is happier and work is more rewarding and the years are richer if life is lived in his name.

Too bad that all have not yet found that out! A young married couple in whose plans the church did not figure explained to a minister who called that they were very much in love with life and did not consider that they needed religion. Unfortunate that some church people had so far lost the Christian radiance that these were led to believe that the gospel would make life less lovely and free and beautiful! Henry Drummond knew better, for he said to a group of students: "I ask you to become Christians not because you may die tonight but because you are going to live tomorrow. I come not to save your souls but to save your lives."

Here, then, is judgment upon men. Here, too, is the Christian doctrine of immortality: it is not just everlastingness — what could be a greater bore? — but Life in his name. Life therefore that links one forever with God. In the early days of our religion a Christian was placed on trial before the Roman governor. " I will banish thee," said the official. " Thou canst not," was the reply, " for my life is hid with Christ in God." " I will take away thy treasures." " Thou canst not," was the answer, " for my treasure is in heaven." " I will drive thee away from man," said the official in desperation, " and thou shalt have no friend left." " Thou canst not," said the Christian, " for I have a Friend from whom thou canst not separate me."

The world does not know what to do with people like that. There is, in fact, nothing that the world can do except to acknowledge that here indeed is the wisdom of God and the power of God. Such fullness of life does not come from blind groping in a book, but from friendship with a Person!

7

"THE WRITTEN CODE KILLS"

A T A CRITICAL period in American life the President
had vigorous ideas regarding what ought to be done
to assure the safety and continuity of the national well-
being. There were many, however, who feared that his
proposals were unconstitutional. It was just at that junc-
ture that there appeared in the *American Bar Association
Journal* an editorial that said: " The spirit is more important than the letter. As long as the spirit of the Constitution is followed, there will be small trouble about the letter, and the great instrument and guarantee of our liberties
is safe. But when the letter is followed in disregard of the
spirit, catastrophe may be near" (Thurman W. Arnold,
The Folklore of Capitalism, page 29. Yale University
Press, 1937).

That is a remarkable statement to appear in a legal
journal. Lawyers are professionally devoted to meticulous
concern about the letter of the law, and not all national
crises have been met in the spirit advocated by the *Journal.*
During his ambassadorship in London at the time of World
War I, Walter Hines Page was greatly embarrassed by the
way in which Lansing conducted the business of the State
Department. He said that Governments were more human than people, yet Lansing went on in an entirely in-

human way, concerned primarily with legal technicalities. "I sometimes wish," wrote Page to Colonel House, "there were not a lawyer in the world. I heard the President say once that it took him twenty years to recover from his legal habit of mind. Well, his administration is suffering from it to a degree that is pathetic and that will leave bad results for one hundred years" (Burton J. Hendrick, *The Life and Letters of Walter H. Page*, Vol. II, page 55. Doubleday, Page & Co., 1922-1925).

It is unfortunate when the spirit of legalistic literalism sets to work upon the Scripture. Concerning a group of literalists who once troubled the American Church, a Scottish observer said, "They're lawyers — just lawyers." If, concerning the Constitution of the United States, "the spirit is more important than the letter," how much more ought interpreters of the Scripture to be aware of that! The Scripture, indeed, carries such a warning concerning itself — and it was a quotation from Scripture that the *Journal* used in setting forth what seemed to the editor the only tenable attitude toward the Constitution. Paul writes to the Corinthians that the letter or "written code kills, but the Spirit gives life" (II Cor. 3:6). The word translated "kills" is an emphatic compound: "kills utterly."

For the belief that the final authority never rests with the letter, we have Jesus' own example. The question was put to him, "Is it lawful to divorce one's wife for any cause?" (Matt. 19:3). The Mosaic law did provide (Deut. 24:1-4) that a man could give his wife "a bill of divorce." This represented something of an advance over more primitive days, when a wife was simply cut loose without any such certificate, as may still be done in Mohammedan countries.

In the Oriental world no misfortune could be greater

than that of an unattached woman. The " bill of divorce " certified that she was no longer the property of the man who had been her husband, and was now free to contract a new alliance. This provision of the Mosaic code was, in our Lord's time, variously interpreted. The strict school of rabbis allowed divorce only on the ground of adultery; the liberal school, on almost any ground. Josephus relates that he had divorced two wives, and for comparatively trivial reasons.

Jesus was challenged then to resolve the issue. Is the Mosaic law to be interpreted strictly or not? He puts the whole matter on an entirely new level, lifting it out of the realm of legalism and literalism. " Have you not read," he asks (Matt. 19:4 f.), " that he who made them from the beginning made them male and female, and said, ' For this reason a man shall leave his father and mother and be joined to his wife, and the two shall become one ' ? " Marriage is ultimately not a matter about which men can legislate. It is a divinely established institution, in which each party gives himself completely to the other. That which has thus been freely bestowed, one is not at liberty to take away and offer to someone else.

Jesus' approach to every problem was vital rather than legal. In directing our study of the Bible, then, the Scripture encourages us to search out the spirit rather than merely look at the letter. It is possible to be thoroughly conversant with the letter of the Bible and miss its spirit completely. A not infrequent complaint of pastors is that their most troublesome members are the ones who can quote the Scripture most lavishly. Young pastors particularly will often admit that, when it comes to a verbatim knowledge of Biblical contents, these difficult parishioners can outdo them. In their concern about the letter these hecklers have allowed the spirit to escape, and their whole attitude is far from that of the New Testament.

Consider what havoc has been wrought by those who found in the Scripture nothing but the letter. Zion City, Illinois, a community of some 6,000 souls, is the headquarters of the Christian Catholic Apostolic Church, an institution founded by the late John Alexander Dowie, who in 1888 came to the United States from Melbourne, Australia. Ignoring the adventure of Columbus and other navigators, Dowie held that the Bible, since it speaks of the universe in terms familiar to the prescientific era, requires us to believe that the world is flat. Dowie seemed more concerned about Biblical ideas of geography than about Biblical ideas of honesty. His financial affairs were questioned, and he became ill and was deposed in 1906.

Dowie was succeeded by Wilbur Glenn Voliva, who was determined at all hazards to maintain the literalistic world view. He maintained a standing offer of $5,000 to anyone who could prove to his satisfaction that the earth was round. At his death in 1942 he had not paid out the money — let us hope that he went " up " to heaven. Voliva's successor, and currently the leader or " overseer " of the movement, is M. J. Mintern. Mintern still insists, on Biblical grounds, that the earth is flat. Rocket photographs taken from fifty-seven miles above the White Sands Proving Ground, in New Mexico, attained sufficient perspective to show the curve in the earth's surface. Unimpressed, Mintern said, " When you have something really worth-while in the way of proof that the earth is spherical, let me know " (*The New York Times*, October 23, 1948).

Literalism in carrying out Biblical injunctions has led to many types of unusual conduct. When a man borrowed all the money he could and ran away with another man's wife, a friend excused him on the ground that " all the wicked things that are happening were prophesied in the Bible, and everything that was prophesied in the Bible somebody has got to act out." A minister was informed by the obstetrician that his wife could be delivered of their child only by Caesarean section. For this the father and husband refused to grant permission on the ground of God's announcement to the woman in Genesis (ch. 3:16), " I will greatly multiply your pain in childbearing; in pain you shall bring forth children." The result was that the wife died and the minister was soon married again — but anyway he was sure he had kept the letter of the Scripture.

No less a person than John Milton (who was unhappily married) defended polygamy on the ground that it was found in the Bible, and " scandalized his Puritan contemporaries by the consistency with which " he urged the examples of Abraham and Jacob " as warrants for polygamy in the Christian Age " (F. D. Maurice, *Social Morality*, page 51. The Macmillan Company, 1886). On the same ground, even Martin Luther reluctantly consented to the bigamous marriage of Philip of Hesse. A man was forbidden to marry a woman with whom he had committed adultery, but Luther held a different opinion: " Even if a man planned the death of the husband in order to marry his widow, he should not be prevented from doing so. He referred to David, who had committed adultery with Bathsheba, caused her husband to be murdered, and then taken her to wife, and still remained a holy man. ' In God's name,' he cries, ' why this harshness against one's fellow men, when God himself did not require it! ' " (ed. Count Hermann Keyserling, *The Book of Marriage*, page 174 f. Blue Ribbon Books, 1931).

In November of 1946, Rev. William Hainsworth, of the

Webster Congregational Church, Dexter, Michigan, announced that he was bidding his congregation good-by for a month in order that he might spend thirty days itinerating from city to city on a trip planned to call attention, not to himself, but to the Bible. People, he said, had come to think of religion as " a slot machine for our loose change." Recalling that Jesus had said, " What ye hear in the ear, that preach ye upon the housetops " (Matt. 10:27, K.J.V.), he announced that his preaching tour would be from roof to roof. He was confident that his project would help in " arousing millions of sleeping Rip Van Christians to the world's desperate need of a wholehearted practice of the principles laid down by Jesus Christ " (*The New York Times,* November 24, 1946).

In denouncing the hypocritical religion of his time, Jesus said, " The harlots go into the kingdom of God before you " (Matt. 21:31). Upon the basis of this, one group of Christians, the Anabaptists of Münster, encouraged sexual promiscuity; that seemed the shortest way into the Kingdom of God! Calling attention to the superficial nature of much that went by the name of religion in his time, Jesus said, " When you pray, you must not be like the hypocrites; for they love to stand and pray in the synagogues and at the street corners, that they may be seen by men " (Matt. 6:5). On the basis of this it has been held that Christians ought not to support or encourage the Salvation Army, since its officers are not infrequently seen praying on the street corners!

The Fourth Evangelist relates that Jesus, at the Last Supper, after singling out the traitor, exclaimed, " What you are going to do, do quickly " (John 13:27). On this passage Cardinal Newman has an " astounding comment . . . as justifying or illustrating the rapid recitation of the words in the Canon of the Mass " (*International Critical Commentary*, T. & T. Clark, Edinburgh, 1928, *in loc.*, refers to *Loss and Gain*, Ch. XX). In I Cor., ch. 7, Paul is concerned to point out that Christianity is not a matter of doing this or of not doing that, and that it need not involve a radical change in outward circumstance: the married person is to go on being married, the slave is to go on being a slave, etc. " Every one should remain in the state in which he was called " (I Cor. 7:20). This surely cannot mean, however, that those engaged in dishonest or dishonorable occupations have no need to change their employment, yet on the basis of this passage manufacturers of idols who had become Christians justified themselves in continuing to earn a living in that way. " Can't you starve? " asks Tertullian (*De idol.* 5:12).

Slavish devotion to the letter of the Scripture has not only led to strange conduct, but has also prompted people to oppose technological improvements and programs for social betterment. A member of a state legislature opposed the plan of his denomination to work out a contributory pension scheme for its ministers. " As a legislator," he said, " I know that everybody is trying to get a pension, and I am afraid this will destroy the American way of life, which encourages people to work hard and save for their old age."

Setting aside the arguments of the legislator, we must note that not everybody wants a pension. When the National Social Security Act went into effect, a group of Mennonites in the legislator's own state expressed unwillingness to accept old-age pensions from the Government. The Mennonite Board of Missions wrote to the Philadelphia office of the Social Security Board expressing the willingness of the members to pay the Social Security taxes "as provided by law. But we have conscientious scruples in regard to receiving the benefits." These objections were based on those Biblical passages which encourage the members of the Christian community to care for their own poor (*The New York Times,* December 2, 1936).

We now think it a civic asset to have the streets lighted at night, and improvements are continually being made along that line: light that throws no shadows is now used on some highways. But street lighting was a comparatively late development; gas illumination was known and understood for many years before it was used in the streets. Good citizens objected to it on the ground that people would stay out all night and catch cold, but also on the Biblical ground that God had divided the light from the darkness (Gen. 1:18) and to interfere in any way with that order would be blasphemous. It may very well be that the extent to which men, women, and young people have now gone in turning night into day is an insult to the creation, which loves variety and is built upon the alternations of activity and repose. Nevertheless, it is certainly using the Scripture wrongly to assert that it forbids the use of a legitimate invention to further human safety.

James Meikle introduced winnowing fans into Scotland in the year 1710, but they were not generally adopted until long afterward, for the reason that the pious, remembering that it was said in the Scripture that " the wind bloweth where it listeth " (John 3:8, K.J.V.), held that those who produced a wind by mechanical means were interfering with the dispensations of Providence. Accordingly, all honorable men would wait for the wind to do their winnowing. It was a similar feeling that led a New York clergyman, when the first oil wells were being drilled in Pennsylvania, to address a petition to the President of the United States, arguing that to extract oil from the earth would be to fly in the face of Providence, which had no doubt stored the oil there as fuel for the predestined burning of the world. When lightning rods were first invented, one man refused to have one placed on his house on the principle that he would scorn to interpose a copper rod between a guilty conscience and an offended God.

To defend ourselves against people who use the Scripture thus two things are required: a better knowledge ourselves of the contents of the Scripture and a genuine understanding of how and why its several parts came into being. Those who regard the letter of the law as final have to be met on their own ground, and the most effective way to overthrow their contention is to be able to cite some other passage which either states the contrary position or puts the whole matter in balance.

Medical men encountered from church people opposition to the use of chloroform, on the ground that while Jesus was hanging on the cross he refused to accept the sop that was offered him. Hence we too should scorn to take anything to lessen pain. Especially violent was opposition to the use of anesthetics in childbirth, for the reason already cited, namely, that it was expressly provided in Gen. 3:16 that in pain women should have to bring forth children. Sir James Young Simpson, professor of midwifery at Edinburgh, was able to meet this argument because he knew his Bible as well as his critics did. Even God, he said, before removing Adam's rib to make a woman, had " caused a deep sleep to fall upon the man " (Gen. 2:21).

In a novel of the eighteenth century, Scripture passages are invoked as ground for ostracizing children born out of wedlock. In *The History of Tom Jones, a Foundling,*

Captain Blifil, who had fathered such a child, argues on Biblical grounds against Squire Allworthy's desire to adopt the infant. The captain contended that "to adopt the fruits of sin was to give countenance to it. He quoted several texts (for he was well read in Scripture), such as: 'He visits the sins of the fathers upon the children'; and 'The fathers have eaten sour grapes and the children's teeth are set on edge,' etc. Whence he argued the legality of punishing the crime of the parent on the bastard" (Henry Fielding, *The History of Tom Jones, a Foundling*, Book II, Chapter II. E. P. Dutton & Co., 1909).

Fortunately, Mr. Allworthy was not awed by this literalism. He answered that "however guilty the parents might be, the children were certainly innocent: that as to the texts he had quoted, the former of them was a particular denunciation against the Jews for the sin of idolatry, of relinquishing and hating their heavenly King; and the latter was parabolically spoken, and rather intended to denote the certain and necessary consequences of sin than express judgment against it. But to represent the Almighty as avenging the sins of the guilty on the innocent was as indecent if not blasphemous, as it was to represent his acting against the first principles of natural justice, and against the original notions of right and wrong which he himself had planted in our minds, by which we were to judge not only in all matters which were not revealed, but even of the truth of revelation itself."

For deliverance from bondage to the letter there is nothing better than ability to match Scripture with Scripture. Better translation also sometimes needs to be invoked. There are at least two places where the King James Bible plays into the hands of those who are suspicious of learning and distrustful of anybody who believes that the spirit is of more importance than the letter. In II Cor. 11:3, Paul, according to this version, expresses his fear lest " your minds should be corrupted from the simplicity that is in Christ." One has heard that quoted by those who feared erudition. It is sometimes hurled at theological students: " Be careful not to let all that so-called learning turn you from the simplicity that is in Christ."

Better translation would have averted the difficulty at this point. The Greek word does not mean such things as appeal to simpletons. It is the opposite, not of learning, but of duplicity, and might be translated " singlehearted devotion." Paul is not afraid that the Corinthians will be corrupted by knowledge: he is afraid that they will be corrupted by that double-minded instability which is not sure what it does want and which tries to seek many ends simultaneously. Paul is arguing for straightforward fidelity, and it is unfortunate that a wrong translation should be allowed to go on creating the false impression it does.

I Timothy 6:20 f. is another passage quoted by those who are suspicious of learning and the spirit: " O Timothy, keep that which is committed to thy trust, avoiding profane and vain babblings, and oppositions of science falsely so called: which some professing have erred concerning the faith." Any knowledge that contravenes inherited prejudices the traditionalist will dismiss as " science falsely so called," and will point out that adherence to this causes wrong notions of faith. Science is therefore in opposition to faith.

Again it is a situation where the seventeenth century translation is misleading. The Greek word rendered " oppositions " is really our English " antitheses "; the word translated " science " is actually " knowledge." The author is warning against "the godless chatter and contradictions of what is falsely called knowledge." It has nothing whatever to do with science or the scientific spirit. It was applicable to the author's immediate situation, and may have either of two references. It may allude to "the endless contrasts of decisions, founded on endless distinctions, which played so large a part in the casuistry of the scribes as interpreters of the law" — the kind of thing our Lord denounced when he spoke of the "tradition of the elders" that had "made void the law of God" (Matt. 15:2, 6 and margin). In that case, it would be a warning to the traditionalist not to put his trust in tradition (*International Critical Commentary, in loc.*).

The other possible reference is to that mass of false beliefs which the Early Church had to combat, beliefs that are together and collectively known as "Gnosticism." The actual Greek word here is *gnosis,* and early in Christian history there appeared those who professed to have extra knowledge, knowledge which in general was made available only to the initiate who had paid the proper sum. In the middle of the second century there was a shipowner of Pontus who undertook to draw a distinction between the God of the Old Testament and the God of the New. He identified the God of the Old Testament with the Gnostic Demiurge who had created the world through a series of emanations. This, he said, could not possibly be the God and Father of Jesus.

This man, Marcion by name, pointed up the contrast in a series of "antitheses," which gave the name to his principal work. There are some, arguing for an exceedingly late date for First Timothy, who suppose that it is specifically aimed at these false doctrines of Marcion, but any of the early stages of Gnosticism would suffice. In which case, the warning would be against that kind of pseudo science circulated by cults such as "New Thought," etc. In either circumstance it becomes clear that the King James Version is quite misleading in throwing suspicion upon science or in setting up opposition between science and faith. Monsignor Knox translates this phrase, "This quibbling knowledge that is knowledge only in name."

It is important also for people to know that literalism is, so far as the Christian Church is concerned, a comparatively recent development. It was not until the conflict with Darwinism arose that churchmen turned to the Scripture as an infallible textbook of science. Charles H. Spurgeon believed the doctrine of evolution to be in conflict with the Genesis story and therefore a thing to be rejected. On October 1, 1861 — *The Origin of Species* had appeared in 1859 — Spurgeon delivered a lecture entitled "The Gorilla and the Land He Inhabits." A stuffed gorilla was on the platform.

Spurgeon said: "I have heard that, if we should admit this gentleman to be our cousin, there is Mr. Darwin, who at once is prepared to prove that our great-grandfather's grandfather's father — keep on for about a millennium or two — was a guinea pig, and that we were ourselves originally descended from oysters, or seaweeds, or starfishes. Now I demur to that on my own account. Any bearded gentleman here, who chooses to do so, may claim relationship with the oyster; and others may imagine that they are only developed gorillas; but I, for my part, believe there is a great gulf fixed between us, so that they who would pass from us to you [turning to the gorilla] cannot; neither can they come to us who would pass from thence. At the same time, I do not wish to hold an argument with a philosopher who thinks himself related to a gorilla; I do not care to claim the honor for myself, but anyone else is perfectly welcome to it " (*Autobiography of Charles H. Spurgeon,* Vol. III, page 54; Vol. IV, page 134. American Baptist Publication Society, n. d.).

Lord Shaftesbury, the great social reformer, took a similar line. He professed to believe in the literal truth and the literal application of every word of the Bible, and said that he had such confidence in it that he would be glad, if he were a rich man, to endow the teaching of science, so sure was his faith that science would confirm the literal truth of the story of the Old Testament. " It will prove the Mosaic creation; the authenticity of the Pentateuch; it will establish the Pentateuch and Noah's ark." This attitude brought him into constant conflict with those who found more or less than he did in the Book. He opposed a manual of geology written by a canon of Manchester and published by the Society for the Promotion of Christian Knowledge. " The slightest concession in respect of the Revealed Word," he wrote, " opens a door which can never be shut, and through which everything may pass " (J. L. and B. Hammond, *Lord Shaftesbury,* page 249. Constable, 1923).

It was in 1861 also that an Oxford theologian, Dean Burgon, set forth the literalist point of view from the pulpit in the following terms: " The Bible is none other than the voice of Him that sitteth upon the throne. Every book of it, every chapter of it, every verse of it, every word of it, every syllable of it (where are we to stop?), every letter of it, is the direct utterance of the Most High. The Bible is none other than the Word of God, not some part of it more, some part of it less, but all alike the utterance of Him who sitteth upon the throne, faultless, unerring, supreme" (quoted by Alan Richardson, *Preface to Bible-Study,* page 27. The Westminster Press, 1944. Also G. J.

Morgan Jones, *The New Testament in Modern Education,*
page 113. Hodder & Stoughton, Ltd., London, n.d.).

It was written in the days of the prophet Hosea (ch.
4:6), " My people are destroyed for lack of knowledge."
The only way to combat this false view of the Bible is by
the introduction of knowledge — the knowledge, for example, that Dean Burgon's statement does not represent
the traditional Christian view. Although the people who
hold it would not like to be called modernists, the idea that
the Scripture is an infallible textbook of science is a de-
cidedly modern one. The literalist point of view is expressed by F. E. Gaebelein in the following words: " Although the Bible is not a textbook of science or history or
any other specific and limited field of knowledge, still it
speaks with authority whenever it touches upon these sub-
jects. Scripture statements having to do with scientific
matters are invariably correct. . . . The Bible is God's inspired Word. Therefore, it cannot be inaccurate; the eternal Father is omniscient and his revelation cannot contain
untruth " (*Exploring the Bible,* page 13 f. Our Hope Publishing Co., 1929).

The argument that a perfect God must have created a
perfect Book cannot be logically sustained. We have to
look at the kind of book God made before deciding what
kind of book he must have made. The fallacy of the argument is apparent when we apply it to the world God made.
God is perfect, and therefore as Creator he must have
made a perfect world. The same argument was employed
by Cardinal Newman to support the doctrine of an infallible Church speaking through an infallible mouthpiece.

This was not the view of Jonathan Edwards. The New
England theologian constantly appealed to the Bible, not
only as the source book of texts for revivalism, but also as

the touchstone by which revivalism was to be tested and proved. Important as the Bible was to him, however, Edwards never considered it as authoritative in any realm except religion. He was fond of the world of nature, but it would never have occurred to him to turn to the Bible as a textbook on science. "The design of the Scripture," he wrote, "is to teach us divinity and not physic and anatomy."

The Reformers believed thoroughly in the Bible as authoritative in matters of faith and conduct, but never had toward it such an idea as Dean Burgon set forth. John Calvin was convinced that the apostles were the "amanuenses of the Holy Spirit, and therefore their writings were to be received as the oracles of God." Nevertheless he was no slavish devotee of the letter as it had been transmitted to him. Noting that the texts of I John 5:7 did not agree, he said that he scarcely dared reach a conclusion. He was uncertain regarding the authorship of II Peter.

On Acts 7:16 he wrote, "It is manifest that there is a mistake in the word Abraham . . . wherefore this place must be amended." On Matt. 27:9 he said, "That the name of Jeremiah has by error crept in here, the thing itself plainly shows, and I do not trouble myself about it." In the preface to one of his commentaries he stated that his purpose was to "edify the children of God, who being not content with the shell wish to penetrate to the kernel."

Men who would use the Bible aright would do well to remember what Augustine said long ago regarding assumptions outside the Christian sphere. "It very often happens," he said, "that there is some question as to the earth or the sky or the other elements of the world . . . respecting which one who is not a Christian has knowledge derived from most certain reasoning or observation, and it is very disgraceful and mischievous, and of all things to be carefully avoided, that a Christian speaking of such matters as being according to the Christian Scriptures should be heard by an unbeliever talking such nonsense that the unbeliever, perceiving him to be as wide from the mark as east from west, can hardly restrain himself from laughing " (quoted by Alex Wood, *In Pursuit of Truth*, A Comparative Study of Science and Religion, page 12. S. C. M., London, 1927).

8

"WE REFUSE TO PRACTICE CUNNING"

IN THE AUTUMN of 1948 the National Society for the Pre-
vention of Blindness, Inc., from its New York office, announced that it was starting a nation-wide survey of the
eye health of children in the American public schools, and
of school conditions regarding light and safety. The survey
was to be initiated on the anniversary of the day when
Francis Scott Key wrote the words of " The Star-spangled
Banner ": " Oh, say, can you see. . . ." We may admire the
cleverness of the publicity experts who thought that up,
but the fact is that Key's words had no reference to sight
as opposed to blindness: it was the object of sight that was
his pressing concern.

Whether we think this legitimate or not, we at least understand what had happened. Oftentimes that kind of use
is made of the Bible, and people generally are not aware
of what is going on. The Fourth Evangelist relates that
Jesus, after the feeding of the five thousand, was involved
in a controversy with the Pharisees regarding the true
bread from heaven. Arguing that Moses had provided all
things needful to sustain the life of the spirit, the Pharisees, pretending to quote Ps. 78:24, " artfully suppress the
nominative (which in the psalm is ' God '), and leave
' Moses ' to be understood " (*Cambridge Bible* on John

6:31). Thus, in order to bolster their position with a reference to Scripture, they "practice cunning," "tamper with God's Word," and so make it seem to say what it does not say.

Matthew and Luke give extensive accounts of our Lord's temptation experience, supplying details that have verisimilitude and must have been supplied by our Lord himself, since he was alone in the desert at the time. The Evangelists represent the temptation as being phrased in Scriptural language: "If you are the Son of God, throw yourself down; for it is written

"'He will give his angels charge of you,'

and,

"'On their hands they will bear you up,
lest you strike your foot against a stone.'"

In times of trial and danger men have known themselves to be sustained by a power not themselves, and Jesus knew more of this than anyone. Yet he would not allow this truth to lead him into a defiance of the law of gravity, and reminded the tempter that in such matters it does not suffice to quote an isolated text. Confidence in the sustaining power of the Unseen must be exercised with reference to the fact that the same Power said, "You shall not tempt the Lord your God" (Deut. 6:16, cited in Luke 4:12).

We must use the Scripture honestly. Paul has set us the example and stated the principle. He writes to the Corinthians: "We have renounced disgraceful, underhanded ways; we refuse to practice cunning or to tamper with God's word, but by the open statement of the truth we would commend ourselves to every man's conscience in the sight of God " (II Cor. 4:2). It is obvious that not all those who quote Scripture do so thus honestly and openly.

The miracle of Jesus is that, across the ages, he has proved himself all things to all men. All sorts of people have found in him the reflection of their own condition and the satisfaction of their own needs. The men of different races have pictured him as being one of them. It has remained, however, for the twentieth century to discover that Jesus was the original Rotarian, the founder of modern business, and the creator of advertising. This phenomenal discovery was made some years ago by Mr. Bruce Barton, who prints upon the flyleaf of his book, " Wist ye not that I must be about my Father's *business?* "

The italics are Mr. Barton's, and represent an unfortunate twist given to an unfortunate translation. The Greek does not say " my Father's business "; it says " the things of my Father " — " did you not know that I must be about the things of my Father? " What are " the things of my Father "? Possibly, the Father's purpose of bringing to men light and leading. As an idiom, it may very well mean " my Father's house " (compare our " I'm going over to my uncle's "). The Revised Standard Version so translates it, " Did you not know that I must be in my Father's house? " (Luke 2:49).

Whether this be a satisfactory rendering or not, one thing is certain: it does not mean what Mr. Barton wants it to mean. He does not tell us that the words were spoken by a twelve-year-old lad at the Temple school — a far cry from there to the New York advertising business over which Mr. Barton presides so successfully. It may very well be, as Frank Kingdon has said, " that this new vision of Jesus has shown some men how fascinating is the whole religious quest." If so, this has been accomplished in spite of Mr. Barton's tampering with the Scripture (Frank Kingdon, *Humane Religion,* page 45. Abingdon Press, c. 1930).

Wrong use of the Scripture is to be charged sometimes even to the clergy. A man came to his minister in great distress because, in another church, he had heard a sermon from the text, " God requireth that which is past." It happened that this was a man with a divided personality: his members were at war with one another. He was extremely introspective, and one of his troubles was an exaggerated sense of guilt. Peccadilloes that should have been long ago forgotten had been brooded upon and magnified until they had assumed the proportion of major crimes. The man could not face present responsibility because he was terrified by memories of past shortcomings.

His case was so baffling that the family physician had referred the patient to a psychiatrist. He was just beginning to make some progress when he was completely undone by the homily on " God requireth that which is past." It was not enough that we should repent, the minister had said: we have to answer for every past omission and are still responsible for all past misdeeds. Not often outside of hospitals are men seen so wrought up as this man was.

The counselor found that there really was such a text: " God requireth that which is past " (Eccl. 3:15), but the context has to be noted. It is part of the passage in which the Preacher is describing life's rhythms and successions: " To every thing there is a season, and a time to every purpose under the heaven " (Eccl. 3:1). The immediate context is: " That which hath been is now; and that which is to be hath already been." The text completes the sentence:

"And God requireth that which is past." To anyone who thoughtfully reads the text in its setting, the meaning is clear. It is simply the vivid Hebrew way of saying that " history repeats itself." " That which hath been is now; and that which is to be hath already been " for the simple reason that God causes seasons and circumstances to repeat themselves. " Require " was used in its strict etymological sense of " recall." God calls back what has been put to flight.

The man seemed greatly relieved by the explanation, but did not really believe it until he was referred to a commentary, where the same interpretation was given in print. No amount of preaching about forgiveness or a new creation or of how God removes our sins as far from us as the east is from the west would have done anything to relieve that man so long as that misused text was confirming his worst fears.

Theological doctrines have sometimes been supported by reference to passages which could be appealed to only by reason of grammatical accident. A minister reports that in his student days in seminary Acts 2:47 was cited in support of the doctrine of predestination: " And the Lord added to the church daily such as should be saved," the implication being that " the ones who should be saved " referred to the elect.

This is just an accident of translation; the Greek means no more than what the Revised Standard Version implies: " The Lord added to their number day by day those who were being saved." The King James translation of Heb. 9:27 was also cited: " It is appointed unto men once to die " — as if the day and hour were foreordained; it is ex-President Truman's " A man will die when his number is up." This is sheer fatalism and is not supported by the true rendering of the Greek: " It is appointed for men to die once."

In Acts 26:28 in the King James Version, King Agrippa is represented as saying to Paul, " Almost thou persuadest me to be a Christian." This has been the basis for many an evangelistic appeal which became stereotyped in the so-called Gospel hymn, " Almost Persuaded." The refrain closes with the pathetic words, " Almost — but lost." For better or for worse, however, this is not what Agrippa was saying. He was not worried about his own soul's condition, but rather was taunting Paul that he thought he could win an argument so easily. What the Greek says is simply, " In a little you think you can make me a Christian." The " in a little " may be either " with a few words " or " in a short time."

One is forced to believe that temperance reform has suffered because in zeal to promote a worthy end men have sometimes allowed themselves to tamper with God's Word. The committee that arranges the International Sunday School Lessons has not been guiltless. There is a passage in Leviticus (ch. 10:8 f.) that reads, " And the Lord spoke to Aaron, saying, ' Drink no wine nor strong drink, you nor your sons with you, when you go into the tent of meeting.' " This was evidently a command to the priests that they should drink no wine while on duty. They should not touch a drop before going to the congregation.

On a Sunday when a temperance lesson was indicated the committee wanted to get an impressive golden text, so they quoted only the words, " Drink no wine nor strong drink." What in the original was directed to the priests, they made to apply to all. What was to be observed under particular circumstances, they made into a universal rule.

To point this out is not to defend strong drink. An age of machine-made speed demands a race of sober men. The point is that it is not fair even for a worthy cause to take a few words of Scripture like that and with them " practice cunning."

One minister went so far as to cite the story of Jesus' turning water into wine (John 2:1 ff.) as proof that Jesus was a foe of wine-drinking, and as a demonstration of his opposition. Citing the saying in John 2:11 that this was " the first of his signs," the clergyman said that this was not a miracle but a remonstrance. He said that " It could not have been a miracle, because a miracle must honor God, must show a moral, and must satisfy the spiritual needs of the Church." Since this miracle, as he thought, did not accomplish any of these worthy ends, it could not have happened.

The clergyman further found it intolerable to think of God as creating wine. " It would be no honor to God to manufacture alcohol," he said. " God is a creator, not a distiller." As an argument, this is not very helpful because fermentation is a natural process that can take place without any aid from man — time will make wine out of grape juice. If God is appealed to as Creator, then he must have, for his own reasons, created this process — and man cannot either wish it away or repeal it.

Instead of performing a miracle, then, Jesus at Cana " performed an object lesson. He made a needed and manly protest against wine-drinking." Citing the instructions to the servants to " fill the jars [rather than the wineskins] with water," the preacher insisted that " Jesus convinced those at the wedding that he was a moral reformer by purposely sending them water when they asked for wine. When the master of ceremonies declared, ' You have kept the good wine until now,' he was referring to water and 'accepting the lesson of Jesus'" (*The New York Times,* probably the last Monday in August, 1935).

Now there can be no doubt that the story of the turning of water into wine is one of the most difficult and perplexing incidents related of our Lord. The minister was right when he sensed a moral difficulty in it. Jesus' miracles generally were wrought, not to impress people, but to relieve human misery and suffering, and give evidence that, in Jesus, the new life in God had for man become a reality. This miracle does not appear to be on that high level, and the only way it can be justified morally is on the ground that to relieve the embarrassment of an improvident host was a worthy use of divine power. Moreover, the prodigality of the miracle raises serious difficulties. The six stone jars are described as holding " each two or three measures." Since a " measure " was approximately ten gallons, that would be 120 to 180 gallons all told. That is a lot of wine! Jesus is generally conservative in the use of miracle. At the feeding of the five thousand, for example, he commanded the disciples, " Gather up the fragments left over, that nothing may be lost " (John 6:12). In view of this divine economy, it is difficult to understand why Jesus would on this occasion only perform so extravagant a miracle. The prodigality of the thing has led some to interpret the saying of the master of ceremonies very differently from the way it was interpreted by the minister above reported: When the " steward of the feast " declared that this was better wine than all the rest, he was revealing the fact that he was already so drunk that he didn't know the difference between water and wine! Hard to think that Jesus would be a party to that kind of debauch.

Probably this story is to be interpreted as a reduction to

narrative, by some unimaginative person, of what Jesus had originally spoken in parabolic terms. He regularly described the Kingdom of Heaven, not as a funeral solemnity, an old folks' home, or a debating society, but as a wedding feast (Matt. 22:3 ff.; Luke 12:36; 14:8). He had also, in one of his sayings, linked wine and wedding joy: " Can the wedding guests mourn as long as the bridegroom is with them? . . . No one puts a piece of unshrunk cloth on an old garment. . . . Neither is new wine put into old wineskins; if it is, the skins burst, and the wine is spilled, and the skins are destroyed; but new wine is put into fresh wineskins, and so both are preserved " (Matt. 9:15-17).

It is not difficult to imagine Jesus, so fond of the imagery of marriage joy, picturing the Kingdom as a realm of such powerful new wine that it simply could not be contained in the old wineskins of Judaism. It is not a long step from that to the narrative as given in the Gospel written last of all. Whether this be the satisfactory solution or not, one thing is certain: no man can honestly use the story as temperance propaganda!

The uncritical use of the Gospel materials, as if they were all upon a single level, has given support to the view that Jesus was a psychiatric case. His opponents among the Pharisees said, " He is possessed by Beelzebul, and by the prince of demons he casts out the demons " (Mark 3:22). Even his family said, " He is beside himself " (Mark 3:21). Two medical men, de Loosten and Binet-Sangle, who used their psychiatric techniques to prove to their own satisfaction that Jesus was a paranoiac, laid great stress upon these two statements regarding the mental condition of Jesus that have come to us from his contemporaries (cf. Albert Schweitzer, *The Psychiatric Study of Jesus,* page 54. Beacon Press, 1948).

The Gospels are remarkably frank in stating the reactions of people who did not understand Jesus, but it is plain that testimony of this kind is not to be set down as an authoritative description of Jesus' mental condition. Obviously, this method of using the Bible — deliberately to foist upon its words, not the meaning they were intended to have, but the meaning you want them to have — can make it say anything. It is worthy of Humpty Dumpty, who, in *Through the Looking Glass*, exclaimed, "When I use a word, it means just what I choose it to mean." By this method of using the Scripture it would be possible even to prove that God does not exist at all. There it is, right in the Bible, in black and white, and written twice: "There is no god." If you don't believe it, look up Ps. 14:1 and Ps. 53:1. Yes, but we must read the entire verse, which gives it a very different turn: "The fool says in his heart, 'There is no god.'"

It is tampering with the Word of God to take a few words of Scripture, tear them loose from their setting, and make them say, not what they meant to say, but what you would like them to say. Some outsiders have been scornful of the Church on the ground that intellectual honesty is a virtue not to be found there. It has never been right to practice cunning, but in a scientific age, when many men acknowledge no allegiance save to truth, no Church and no good cause can hope to prosper by using the Scripture dishonestly.

Men of good motives have sometimes twisted a verse of Scripture to suit their purposes. In the last century, W. F. Hook, a High-Church divine, preaching before the young Queen Victoria, had for his text the words, "Hear the church," and proceeded to tell the youthful monarch that this meant she should submit to all the dogmas of the High

Anglican philosophy. But when the words are seen in their setting, it is apparent that they can mean nothing of the kind. Jesus is represented as describing how to deal with offenders. There are some who consider that this reflects the practice of excommunication, borrowed from Judaism by the Early Church, rather than Jesus' own disposition toward the recalcitrant. In any case, Jesus is reported to have said: " Take one or two others along with you. . . . If he refuses to listen to them, tell it to the church; and if he refuses to listen even to the church, let him be to you as a Gentile and a tax collector " (Matt. 18:16 f.).

A phrase from an " if " clause is taken from its setting and changed into a command! Commercial agencies sometimes resort to this kind of cunning. A magazine was trying to get church advertisements, and emblazoned on the prospectus was what purported to be a Biblical text, taken from The Book of Ruth: " And I thought to advertise . . . before the inhabitants " (ch. 4:4). The actual passage is: " I thought to advertise thee [here, " advertise " is used in its original sense of " notify "], saying, Buy it before the inhabitants, and before the elders " — which meant that the matter of disposing of the inheritance was to be settled before the authorities and not in private.

The magazine, however, twists it so as to make it an injunction to the churches that they purchase some display advertising. Similarly, a news magazine, in an advertisement especially directed toward the clergy, stated: " Wars and Rumors of Wars . . . False Prophets Deceive the Very Elect." This was calculated speedily to bring forth ministerial subscriptions to a magazine devoted to rapid dissemination of news about the troubled world.

Nor is it a right use of Scripture to treat it all as if it were upon the same level, and its examples and injunctions to be applied indiscriminately. Rev. Henry Smith, commonly called "the silver-tongued preacher" of seventeenth century England, is said to have "preached a sermon on *Sarah's* nursing of *Isaac*, and thereupon grounded the general doctrine that it was the duty of all mothers to nurse their own children, allowing dispensation to such who were insufficienced by weakness, want of milk, or any avouchable impediment. He pressed the application without respect of persons high or low, rich or poor, one with another" (George Adam Smith, *Modern Preaching and the Old Testament*, page 244, note 1. Hodder & Stoughton, Ltd., n. d.).

We may distinguish also what may be called the indiscriminate use of Scripture — that is to say, applying the words of the Bible to some situation purely on the basis of a verbal coincidence, without regard to the context or original meaning of the passage. Charles Lamb used to tell of having seen an epitaph, in the Islington churchyard, of an infant "Aetatis four months," with the inscription, "Honor thy father and thy mother that thy days may be long in the land" (Will D. Howe, *Charles Lamb and His Friends*, page 328. Bobbs-Merrill Company, 1944).

A young husband informed his wife, "I don't want to wipe dishes; it isn't a man's work." To which the young wife replied with a quotation from II Kings 21:13: "And I will wipe Jerusalem as a man wipeth a dish, wiping it, and turning it upside down." It is said of Dorothy Drew, grandchild of W. E. Gladstone, that she was not at all fond of getting up in the morning. Her grandfather practiced early rising himself and believed in it for others. He had a serious talk with her about it. "'But,' said the little maid, 'the Bible says we ought not to get up early.' Mr. Gladstone, who knew his Bible as well as anyone, was greatly puzzled, for he had never heard of such a text. At last the little girl found the words and showed him: ' Woe unto them that rise up early in the morning ' " (*Expository Times*, January, 1934, page 174).

Yes, it is in the Bible right enough. It is one of the prophetic utterances of Isaiah, the prophet of holiness. But we must not forget to read the entire verse, which is: " Woe unto them that rise up early in the morning, that they may follow strong drink " (Isa. 5:11). A ladies' church auxiliary circulated what it called " A Bible Cake Recipe." Upon the payment of ten cents, one was given a formula for making " two wonderful cakes." The baker was to take " 3 cups of Jeremiah 6:20," " 2 cups of I Samuel 30:12," " 2 teaspoonfuls of Amos 4:5," etc., etc., the whole to be treated as recommended in Proverbs 23:14.

Men of New Testament times read the Old Testament in the light of what they knew about Christ, and found that the Old Testament made unexpected reference to him. In the light of Christ's death on the cross, the Suffering Servant passage in Isa., ch. 53, took on new meaning: It was *Jesus*, said the Church, who had " borne our griefs and carried our sorrows "; it was *Jesus* who had been " wounded for our transgression " and " bruised for our iniquities "; it was *Jesus* who " poured out his soul to death, and was numbered with the transgressors." So the Old Testament phrases having to do with Messiah are applied to Jesus. He is " Son of Man," " Son of David," " Immanuel." The Messianic expectation finds in him a fulfillment of which the prophets only vaguely dreamed.

It is right that the Old Testament should be so read, and Jesus linked up with all that was finest and best in the hopes and aspirations of his people. It is a mistake, however, to try to find in every Old Testament detail some obscure allusion to Christ, as did the early commentator who saw a prediction of the Virgin birth in the saying, "He grew up . . . like a root out of a dry ground" (Isa. 53:2); or to base the doctrine of the perpetual virginity of Mary on the saying in Ezek. 44:2: "And he said to me, 'This gate shall remain shut; it shall not be opened, and no one shall enter by it; for the Lord, the God of Israel, has entered by it; therefore it shall remain shut.'"

Mark 14:51 f. relates that, on the night when Jesus was arrested, "a young man followed him, with nothing but a linen cloth . . . and ran away naked." It is generally supposed that this is an autobiographical note, and that the young man was Mark himself. The reasoning is that it seems to serve no other conceivable purpose, and that such a circumstance would have fixed itself indelibly upon the young man himself. Yet this kind of Scripture interpretation would insist that this happened because Amos had said, concerning a forthcoming time of hardship in Israel, "And he who is stout of heart among the mighty shall flee away naked in that day."

Let us therefore not be overawed by anyone who says, "It's in the Bible." The Bible is a book that can be misused by the uninformed, tampered with by the cunning, and turned to evil ends by those who deliberately pervert the truth. What we require, then, is to understand as much as possible about the setting of the various parts of the Bible, and to sit down humbly before them and let them speak to us as they spoke to those who first benefited from them. This is not easy. It requires study, investigation, the use of introductions, commentaries, and helps of various kinds.

Dwight L. Moody did not have very much use for the world of books. William Lyon Phelps said that he would prefer a knowledge of the Bible without a college education to a college education without the Bible. But there is no reason why the man of God should shut out of his mind any realm of learning, and Moody has been criticized for his indifference to the great literature of the world. Gamaliel Bradford, for example, says, " How much Moody missed by not knowing the hopes and fears of the human heart as expressed in, let us say, the plays of Shakespeare! "

But Mr. Moody did know the Bible, and he knew how it ought to be read. He insisted that in interpreting any passage we " must understand whom it is written to " — by which he meant that there were parts of the Bible that were directed to the saved and parts to the unsaved. " Very often," he wrote, " a sinner will get hold of some comforting word addressed to a Christian and he will go and take comfort in it when he has no right to any more than I would have a right to read someone's letters."

One cannot get the full import of the four Gospels unless he knows something of the different groups of people they were intended to reach. One cannot understand the true significance of Paul's letters to the Corinthians unless he knows of the conditions prevailing in Corinth at the time when they were written. One is hopelessly befuddled in studying the Apocalypse unless he has some acquaintance with its background of suffering and persecution, and the need for concealing dangerous truths from the contemporary Roman oppressors. The informed student is the one who knows how to use the Scripture aright and not practice cunning.

9

"KEEP YOURSELVES FROM IDOLS"

THE RUSSIAN CHRISTIAN exile, Nicholas Berdyaev, has said that "many old idols are overturned in our times, but many new idols are being created." He believed that this is apparent in "science, in art, in political, national life." He considered, for example, that "Communism is an extreme form of social idolatry" (quoted in *Religion in Life,* autumn, 1948, page 504). It will be the contention of this chapter that religious people too have set up a new idol. The Reformation banished idols from the churches and even destroyed works of art that were replete with loveliness and beauty. Now the Bible itself has been set up as an object of worship!

The First Epistle of John closes with the words, "Little children, keep yourselves from idols" (I John 5:21). The books of the New Testament were not written in the order in which they appear in our English versions, and there are some who suppose that I John was the last book to have been written — in which case this warning would come to us with all the solemnity and impressiveness of the latest voice of the Scripture. As addressed to Christians of the first or second century, it no doubt had reference to "the delusive and vain idols of the Cerinthian Gnosticism," which spoke in terms of aeons and emanations and held these to be sacred. The injunction intends to forbid

" all things and everything which may be opposed to the God revealed in Christ and to his worship in spirit and in truth " (C. J. Ellicott, *A Commentary for English Readers, in loc.*).

As applied to a later age, those are right who see in it a prohibition of Mariolatry as well as the worship of the pope, the saints, or the Church. Each congregation tends to set up its own objects of veneration, and this forbids " anything that occupies the place due to God." One Protestant family opposed the erection of a new church building in the community. The need was admitted, but they said they did not want to see the old one torn down because their father, a carpenter, had fashioned the doors! Thus a church building itself can sometimes become an object of veneration. There can be no doubt either that the Bible has by some been made into a fetish. This is evidenced in those homes where someone is shocked if a member of the household inadvertently places another book on top of the Bible.

In accordance with this veneration of the Bible itself, it is not surprising to find that it has sometimes been used as a book of magic. It has been hardly more than a century since the " Trial by Bible and Key " was one of the techniques of administering justice. The procedure was as follows: " A Bible is procured, and the wards of a key being placed in or about the middle, the book is tied so that the key, on being suspended by the bow, will sustain the weight of the book; a thread is fastened to the bow or the key, and each party in succession places the thread on his or her finger, thus suspending the book therefrom. Some incantation is pronounced, and the Bible is expected to revolve if the party be guilty, and remain stationary if innocent."

This is somewhat like the ordeal by water: if a person sank, he was innocent; if he floated he was guilty! *The Times* of London related on January 21, 1842, that Louisa, " wife of J. Stebbings, was examined by Bible and key before the mayor and magistrates of Yarmouth, being charged with having robbed the house of William J. Presant. On the evidence thus procured, Louisa was sent to trial and ultimately found guilty " (*The New York Times*, February 24, 1942).

This was thought to have been the last such ordeal, but when the story was reprinted in 1942, a correspondent wrote in to say: " I was present at a similar performance in the late 1860's in the home of my father and mother in London. They had in their employ an illiterate Norfolk girl, and I was allowed to go into the kitchen to write a letter home for her. However, she never seemed to feel sure that I had set down faithfully her exact words — hence her resort to the Bible and the key method."

People have sometimes thought that the Bible could be appealed to to settle a problem as one might do by tossing up a coin. There was a time when any question could be settled by opening the Bible at random, putting your finger blindly upon some passage, and considering that the message found there was a special divine oracle intended for you under those circumstances. A minister grew up among people who practiced this kind of Bible magic. Once when he was going on a long journey, which had been undertaken with some misgivings, he opened his Bible the first night in the Pullman berth, hoping that the first verse his eyes lighted upon would give him courage. What he read was this: " To-day shalt thou be with me in paradise."

The story is told of a young lady who was being wooed by a huge and somewhat uncouth young man. It was a question as to whether she ought to marry him. Her mother was a believer in this magical use of the Bible and had her daughter pick out a passage in this random fashion. The verse she hit upon was this: " The Lord that delivered me out of the paw of the lion, and out of the paw of the bear, he will deliver me out of the hand of this Philistine " (I Sam. 17:37). It is good to know that her affections proved stronger than her superstitions, and she married him anyhow.

One has heard also of the youth in search of guidance for his lifework. Opening the Bible at random, he read that Judas " went and hanged himself." The result of his second try was even more alarming: " Go, and do thou likewise." This magical use of the Scripture has been by no means confined to those about whom one hears in anecdotes. It has been practiced by some able and saintly people, including leaders of the Wesleyan revival.

In the early days of the Great Awakening, when it was necessary for George Whitefield to return to London, he " begged Wesley to come to Bristol and carry on the great movement he had begun. Wesley resorted to his lot-finding again to discover whether he should go, but with an amusing result. The first Scripture he obtained in this way was: ' Get thee up into this mountain, and die in the mountain whither thou goest up.' Not liking this, he appealed to the Fetter Lane meeting to take up the inquiry. They tried, and turned up: ' Son of man, behold I take from thee the desire of thine eyes at a stroke, yet thou shalt not mourn nor weep, neither shall thy tears run down.' Not satisfied even yet, the brethren tried once more, only to learn: ' And Ahaz slept with his fathers, and they buried him in the city, even in Jerusalem.' In spite of this, to Wesley's credit be it said, he went to Bristol " (A. D. Belden,

George Whitefield, the Awakener, page 66. Sampson Low, Marston & Co., Ltd., 1930).

At critical periods in his life, Lord Shaftesbury was accustomed to open the Bible at random and take the first passage he came to as a divine message. Catherine Booth terminated her love affair with her irreligious cousin when she opened the Bible to II Cor. 6:14. St. John Ervine adds: "We may wonder what would have been her attitude to the young man if she had chanced to open St. Paul's First, instead of his Second, Epistle to the Corinthians, and in the seventh chapter had read the fourteenth verse" (St. John Ervine, *God's Soldier: General William Booth,* Vol. I, page 24. The Macmillan Company, 1924).

The question was debated in the Middle Ages as to what would happen to a mouse that crept into church and ate part of the consecrated host: would it attain immortality? Those who venerate the Bible now puzzle themselves over what would happen to an animal that ate some of the sacred pages. Sir Wilfred Grenfell relates that at one point on the Labrador, "some sacrilegious pigs which had been brought down to fatten on the fish, driven to the verge of starvation by the scarcity of that article, had broken into the church illicitly one night, and had actually torn up and eaten the Bible." In reply to inquiry, he says, "I gave it as my opinion that it would be no sin to eat the pork of the erring quadrupeds." He might even have called attention to Jer. 15:16: "Thy words were found, and I did eat them" (Sir Wilfred Grenfell, *Forty Years for Labrador,* page 100. Houghton Mifflin Company, 1932).

During World War II there was a deliberate attempt on the part of commercial interests to capitalize on the superstitious belief that the Bible worn over the heart might serve as a talisman, protecting the wearer from harm.

Stores near Army camps featured " the Heart-Shield Bible, with gold-plated engraved 20-gauge steel front cover; fits the pocket over the heart; protect his heart! may deflect bullet, shrapnel, bayonet; in addition to the life-saving feature, the Heart-Shield Bible will be the most cherished souvenir of this world's worst war." Samples were shown with various legends on the cover: " God's Weapon "; " May this keep you from harm "; " God bless you." The Roman missal could be obtained in the same format.

The New York Times for February 19, 1945, carried a dispatch from Washington containing a War Department announcement that " a prayer book saved the life of Pvt. John W. Monohon, Detroit infantryman, when a bullet gouged the cover and ' ricocheted off the prayers,' leaving only a red mark on his chest." This, however, does not appear to have been a steel-jacketed prayer book — it was just the thickness of the little volume that did the work.

Actually, steel-bound Bibles do not appear to have been very effective bullet stoppers, since the sheet of steel was so thin as to have little effect upon a bullet that had not spent its force — except to splatter it and cause it to make a larger and uglier wound than it would otherwise have done. The *Pittsburgh Post-Gazette* for January 20, 1945, reported that " the Shields of Faith Company . . ., which sells steel-covered Bibles and Catholic prayer books to members of the armed forces, was accused by the Federal Trade Commission in Washington yesterday of ' false, exaggerated and misleading ' claims in its sales campaign:

" Not only are the ' shields ' incapable of ' deflecting bullets, pieces of shrapnel, and bayonet thrusts,' as the FTC charges the company has claimed, the metal cover, instead of being a protection, creates an additional hazard because a bullet passing through it would be distorted by the impact on the metal, and upon entering the body would cause a much more serious and painful wound."

A chaplain reported that an officer, nervous and brooding after some harrowing experiences in battle, was rummaging through his bag and came upon a New Testament which he did not recognize. Opening it, to see whether the owner's name was in it, he read: "My darling husband, If you are lonely, troubled, or confused, may you turn to this for guidance and comfort and know I'm with you in hope and prayer. Your loving wife." The officer stated that he had then read some portions of the Book, and that they had made a new man out of him. "I thank God," he said, "for the power of his Word and for the wonderful wife he has given me."

Not all stories about the uses to which the Bible was put during the war have so happy an ending. A mother, helping her son to sort his clothing, found in the breast pocket of his old Army uniform the Bible she had sent him. "Did you read it?" she asked. "Yes, Mother." "How far?" "From cover to cover." "Open it to page three," said the mother, thrusting the Testament at him accusingly. There he found a five-dollar bill. "I put it there when I sent the Bible," she said.

Some seem to make a fetish of the Bible's format, and determine the worth of a version by the color of its binding. Devotees of a particular version sometimes exhibit toward it an attitude that makes it impossible for them to get help from any other. A preface to a Bible "Made for the Gideons by the National Bible Press" says of the King James translators and their work: "That the hand of God rested firmly on these able and sincere men during the nearly four years of their labors is highly manifest. Of the beloved translation which they produced, it has been fittingly said, ' No other book of any kind has so affected the life of a people as this Authorized Version has affected the life of the English-speaking people.'

"Within forty years of the publishing of the first edition in 1611 the King James had displaced other versions and became *the* Bible in English. In the affections of all devout persons it has never yielded that predominant place, which is its right by its sterling worth.

"On the spiritual side, as the true Word of God, it is the most precious thing this world affords. On the secular side, it is indeed a priceless treasure, since it has set the pattern of our language, and has inspired and influenced much of the best in our literature. Companion and guide of our fathers, cherished possession of today, sacred heritage of our children, it is indeed THE BOOK OF BOOKS."

This kind of unreason has closed the minds of many to all new truth, and made them look with uneasiness, suspicion, and distrust upon any other version, even where new light has been shed upon what the original Greek New Testament said. So idolatrous have people become in their attitude toward the King James Bible that even an obvious misprint has been sanctified. In Matt. 23:24 this version describes the Pharisees as "blind guides, which strain at a gnat, and swallow a camel." Straining *at* a gnat does not make sense. "Straining *out* a gnat" is what the translators intended, but a printer is responsible for the strange corruption which nobody these three hundred years has had the courage to correct. Is there in all history any other case of a printer's errors being hallowed?

The writer was scheduled to speak in an Eastern city on the Revised Standard Version of the New Testament. Upon arrival at the place of meeting he was informed that a letter had been received for him. Since he was scheduled to be there only for the hours necessary to go and come, he was not expecting any mail to reach him there. Word that a letter had come caused some uneasiness, since only his family knew where he was and they had that day communicated with him elsewhere. It must be an extremely urgent communication.

When the letter was handed to him, anxiety turned to puzzlement: the handwriting was wholly strange and the postmark was that of a small town of which he had hardly even heard. The letter, written in pencil, was signed: " A Bible Student." It enclosed a newspaper notice of the gathering the present writer was to address, and stated: " Noticing the enclosed article, as, a baptised Presbyterian, I suggest you study the 22nd chapter — Revelation especially the last several verses, if you have *Faith* enough to *believe* in Word of *God!* Note what he says he *will do to those,* who *add* or *take away* of his words *a wise person will try to avoid annoying God.*"

The letter furnished a somewhat amusing introduction for the talk which that evening was delivered to a religiously literate audience, and for the writer's unexpected help in that respect the speaker was grateful. Subsequent reflection, however, suggests that such a letter — in spite of its being anonymous — ought not to be treated lightly, since it represents an attitude that is more widespread than some suspect. The letter writer styles herself (it is not clear whether the author was a man or woman but the handwriting suggests the feminine critic) " A Bible Student." She no doubt believes herself to be thoroughly conversant with God's Word, and devoted to it to the point where she is willing — without standing up and being named! — to defend it from what she regards as the assault of its enemies.

A theological professor would probably be a good deal more afraid of " annoying God " than she is. Many of the religiously uninformed, however, take her at her word and consider her an authority on the Bible. Theological professors they — and she — regard with suspicion, as men somehow determined to destroy the authority of the Word, to the study of which their whole lives and careers are devoted. So far as vested interests are concerned, the professional student has a good deal more at stake than the letter writer in maintaining the authority, integrity, and significance of the Bible. Nevertheless, she wanted to put him in the position of a destroyer of it!

Revelation 22:18 f. does pronounce a curse upon anyone who tampers with " the words of the prophecy of this book: if any one adds to them, God will add to him the plagues described in this book, and if any one takes away from the words of the book of this prophecy, God will take away his share in the tree of life and in the holy city, which are described in this book." Since this passage occurs in a document that brings to a close the New Testament as it is familiar to English readers, " A Bible Student " assumes that it refers to the whole of the Scripture. When Revelation was first written, however, it circulated — in the manner of all ancient documents — on a single papyrus roll, by itself. The curse therefore seems in the first instance intended specifically for the book of Revelation. In making it applicable to the whole of the Bible, it is evident that it is " A Bible Student " and not the professor who has added something to God's Book.

It ought next to be noted that these are human words,

rather than words of God. Revelation 22:17 contains one of the most gracious and precious promises in all the Scripture: "The Spirit and the Bride say, 'Come.' And let him who hears say, 'Come.' And let him who is thirsty come, let him who desires take the water of life without price." If a lofty and compelling utterance like that is followed immediately by the curse above reported, we have to assume either that God can be startlingly anti-climactic and unreasonable, or that there has been a change of speaker. The curse is evidently the work of the man who put the book together. Some acquaintance with ancient literature suggests that this was the way in which early writers sought to protect the integrity of their books.

Our modern books print in the front some such threat as this: "All rights in this book are reserved. No part of the text may be reproduced in any form without written permission of the publishers, except brief quotations used in connection with reviews in magazines or newspapers." Even translations of the Bible are copyright "to insure purity of text." Lacking both the protection of the copyright laws and the fixity of a book printed and bound, the ancients had no way of safeguarding the integrity of the manuscript except by appending some such threat. In the case of the last book in the Bible, this was particularly necessary because the work came into being in a time of persecution and was "exposed to peculiar danger, and the minute and admirable connection . . . might be disturbed or obscured by the change of even a single word" (J. A. Bengel, *op. cit., in loc.*).

It is of further significance to discover that this threat is in the Old Testament manner. In Deut. 4:2, Moses says to the people of Israel, "You shall not add to the word which I command you, nor take from it; that you may keep the commandments of the Lord your God which I command you." So also, after Moses' second ascent into the Mount, his address to the people concludes, "Everything that I command you you shall be careful to do; you shall not add to it or take from it" (Deut. 12:32). At a crucial moment in the life of Israel, Jeremiah heard God saying: "Thus says the Lord: Stand in the court of the Lord's house, and speak to all the cities of Judah which come to worship in the house of the Lord all the words that I command you to speak to them; do not hold back a word" (Jer. 26:2).

It is evident that in these instances the threat is addressed to the hearers of the spoken word rather than merely to the copyists. Those to whom the divine injunction comes are to carry it out fully: they are not to distort it by omitting some of its emphases, nor are they to corrupt it by appending observations of their own. If the threat in Revelation is in the Old Testament tradition, then it is directed to the heart and conscience of each reader: Have we obeyed the injunctions of this book? Have we the kind of character that will be faithful unto death? Have we suffered any kind of torment rather than prove faithless to the Lord of love?

Also, can "A Bible Student" be sure of precisely what the curse said in the first place? Ancient writing materials were fragile, and the original of this perished long ago. For fourteen hundred years, until the invention of printing, every copy that anywhere existed was written out by fallible human hands. A student of the old manuscripts has said, "In this very interdict, about the not adding or taking away, I have noticed twenty-four varieties of reading introduced by copyists" (critical note in J. A. Bengel, *op. cit., in loc.*).

There is the further problem of the whole significance of the book in which the curse appears. A distinguished Scottish scholar of the last generation has said that it "might be called the most Christian book in the New Testament. Written at a time of persecution and conflict, every feeling in it is strained and intense; there is a passion in all it asserts of Christ, in all its longings for Christ, which can hardly be paralleled elsewhere." Many thoughtful students, on the other hand, have felt that it left something to be desired. Its spirit of vindictiveness and exultant triumph over foes is not the spirit of One of whom I Peter 2:23 says, "When he was reviled, he did not revile in return; when he suffered, he did not threaten."

The Apostolic Fathers do not comment upon it, nor did John Calvin. Martin Luther expressed a strong aversion to it. He did not believe that its threats were in line with the promised gift of the Holy Spirit, nor that its outlook was either apostolic or prophetic. "A sufficient reason why I do not esteem it highly," he said, "is that Christ is neither taught nor recognized in it, which is what an apostle ought before all things to do." Rejecting it from the true body of Scripture, Luther printed it as an appendix to his New Testament. Zwingli, another of the Reformers, regarded it as "not a Biblical book."

In referring to the twenty-second chapter of Revelation, the letter writer was accepting what somebody had added to the Bible. That is to say, there were no chapter divisions at all in the original Revelation. These were not devised until the thirteenth century, when it occurred to someone that the Biblical material might be more conveniently studied if it were broken up into manageable portions. The chapter divisions were then introduced, the attempt being to make the chapters approximately equal in length. A classical volume on preaching says, " In fixing the limits of the text and the context, the preacher needs to be warned against a false reliance on the chapter and verse divisions in the Authorized Version " (A. E. Garvie, *The Christian Preacher,* page 390. Charles Scribner's Sons, 1921).

The unthinking attitude which some have toward the familiar version of the Bible has actually led to the beatification of the king under whose auspices it came into being. Many who would be horrified at the suggestion that there was any hagiology in Protestantism nevertheless refer to the " Saint James Version." This has actually appeared in print, in a Hearst newspaper. One college speech teacher got her saints a little confused, and was sure that her students in quoting the Bible should always use the " Saint John Version."

The canonization of James has doubtless been aided by the " Epistle Dedicatory " still carried in many — but not all — editions of the King James Version. The translators must have kept their fingers crossed when they wrote that! The only way to offset it, apparently, is a little historical research into the character of James, who was far from being a saint, and who authorized a fresh translation of God's Word because he thought it would heighten the prestige of James and help to draw attention away from some of his failures.

In spite of this, the idea still persists that the King James Version somehow has a divine approval not granted to other translations. A college president in the South said that a mountain preacher had assured him that " God told King James to write the Bible and he did it. The devil inspired the other one, the American Version." Another college president relates that he had heard a traveling man, extolling the King James Version, say, " God gave his law to Adam, and the devil came along with a revised version." The Mr. and Mrs. Fearings of the Church are always afraid that somebody is trying to destroy the Bible. The real situation is that they, closing their minds against fresh insights into God's truth, have become idolaters of it.

10

"IN HIM ALL THINGS HOLD TOGETHER"

A T THE PARC DE SAINT-CLOUD; in the suburbs of Paris, the International Bureau of Weights and Measures has its headquarters. There is enshrined the standard measuring stick of the world. It is a bar of platinum iridium on whose polished surface are two fine lines. When the temperature of the bar is zero degrees centigrade, the distance between those lines is precisely one meter. Other measuring sticks are checked against this bar. In inches it is 39.37, and even the British verify their standard yard by it.

This criterion for all measurements is well protected. To guard it from disturbances on the surface of the earth, it is kept far underground. To reach it, one has to descend three flights of cellar stairs and be admitted through two iron doors. Inside these barriers there is a triple case of glass, hard rubber, and wood. This carefully preserved meter has hitherto served the world well, but scientists are now looking for something better. Modern techniques have caused its accuracy to be called in question. Compared with what precision instruments are now able to accomplish, the lines on the bar appear coarse and irregular.

Also, its permanence is now a matter of concern. In the atomic age all man-made measuring sticks, including this one, could be destroyed. It is therefore held that man's fundamental unit of measure should not be anything arbitrary and man-made, but rather something that is inherent in the universe. A cosmic measuring stick, with an accuracy of one part in a hundred million, has been discovered. Pure gold, which has an atomic weight of 197, is placed in an atomic pile, bombarded by a storm of neutrons, and thus transmuted into a single mercury isotope with an atomic weight of 198. This one-isotope mercury gives off green light waves of marvelous uniformity, so that here at last is a measuring stick unchanging and indestructible.

Dealers in real estate too have been looking for more permanent ways of bounding their properties. An organization concerned with the preservation of historic sites has for its motto, "Remove not the ancient landmark which your fathers have set" (Prov. 22:28). The Hebrew proverb, however, was not concerned with the retention of old buildings. The reference was to those stones or heaps of stones or trees with a pattern cut into the bark which were intended to fix the limits of a man's farm or field or estate. In Egypt, boundary stones were regularly swept away by inundations of the Nile. Hebrew law invoked a curse upon anyone who surreptitiously removed a neighbor's landmark.

Properties used always to be bounded by landmarks: creeks and bridges and roads and trees and walls and boulders. Sometimes now the base line is determined by its relation, not to any visible landmarks, but to a meridian of latitude. It is not otherwise in measuring spiritual attainment and mapping out of the homeland of the soul.

A church school teacher contends that the Bible in the King James Version is the standard by which everything in the life as well as the literature of religion is to be judged. Persons holding this point of view resent it if any new information comes to light about God's Word. They feel that the old landmarks have been taken away, leaving them bewildered and alone in a world they never made.

Far better, however, to have a cosmic yardstick and one that is indestructible! That, according to the New Testament, is precisely what Jesus Christ is. Concerning him, Paul writes to the Colossians (ch. 1:17), " He is before all things, and in him all things hold together." He does not say that Christ *was* before all things, but that Christ *is* before all things. Here, as best our human speech can manage it, is a striving after timelessness. When God revealed himself to Moses, he said, " I AM WHO I AM " (Ex. 3:14). With God, everything is one perpetual here-and-now. So, says Paul, is it with Jesus: he is before all things, and in him all things hold together.

Everything even in the Scripture has to be judged by what Jesus was and did. The Reformers made this the principle upon which they decided whether books were or were not to be admitted to the canon. " That which does not teach Christ," said Luther, " is not apostolic, though Peter or Paul should have said it; on the other hand, that which preaches Christ would be apostolic, even if it had come from Judas, Annas, Herod, and Pilate " (cited by J. A. McClymont, *New Testament Criticism,* page 14. Hodder & Stoughton, Ltd., 1913).

The Early Church read the Hebrew sacred writings in the light of what it knew about Jesus. At a time when there was no New Testament, Christian preachers turned to the Law and the Prophets for passages descriptive of Jesus' life and ministry. The apostles used what we know as the Old Testament as the basis for their sermons about Christ. The prophets were, in the first instance, primarily concerned about their own time and situation. The first Christian teachers, however, believed that, under the influence of the Eternal Spirit, they often said more than they knew, and that their utterances found true fulfillment as applied to Christ.

Several New Testament books are especially concerned with Jesus' relationship to the Old Testament. Matthew's Gospel is evidently given its present form in deliberate reference to the writings that bear the name of Moses. As there are five books of the Law, so there are five sections of discourse material in Matthew. As Moses brought the Law down from Mount Sinai, so Jesus goes up into the mountain to deliver the Sermon which is the constitution of God's new order. As there are long addresses of Moses in the Pentateuch, so the sayings of Jesus are grouped in continuous discourses by Matthew.

The opening section of the Gospel of John is no doubt in conscious imitation of the opening book of the Old Testament. Genesis starts by telling what transpired "in the beginning." So the Fourth Evangelist indicates that with the incarnation there began a new creation. " In the beginning was the Word. . . . And the Word became flesh and dwelt among us, . . . the law was given through Moses; grace and truth came through Jesus Christ." The Epistle to the Hebrews is concerned to exhibit Christ's superiority to Old Testament worthies. He is greater than Moses and Aaron and Melchizedek.

D. L. Moody was fond of saying that he believed all parts of the Bible to be of equal worth, and all Scripture on exactly the same level. "We want to believe the whole Bible," he said. "We want to take the whole if it, from Genesis to Revelation " (J. S. Ogilvie, *Ten Days with D. L. Moody*, page 10. 1885). Referring to the fact that the New Testament frequently quotes the Old, he says he believes in Noah's Flood and Lot's wife " as I believe the sermon on the Mount " (*Ibid.*, page 21). " Let us," he says (*Ibid.*, page 31), "take the Book, and let us believe it from beginning to end — every word true — and the words we can't understand, let us believe them."

That was no doubt what Mr. Moody believed that he believed. His actual practice was different from, and much better than, his creed. He was sure that the whole Bible had to be understood in the light of what Jesus was and what he did on the cross. In an address on Bible study Moody quoted with approval Bishop Stevens, of Philadelphia: " Don't study it with your little red light of Methodism or your little blue light of Presbyterianism, or the light of the Episcopal Church, but just the light of Calvary " (*Ibid.*, page 30).

Here is help for those who are uneasy regarding the many new discoveries about the Bible that have come to attention in the past hundred years. Manuscripts far older than those in use for Reformation Bibles are now in our possession. They reveal what the Scripture said before fallible human copyists made mistakes, and so at many points we are compelled to correct the text of the Bible by bringing it in line with what is known about the original. For example, the snake-handling passage, mentioned in our opening chapter, is now revealed to be no true part of Mark's Gospel.

New sayings of Jesus have turned up on frail papyrus leaves. Fresh discoveries have been made about Biblical vocabulary, so that familiar terms are sometimes given different connotations. It has become clear, also, that many books of the Bible have reached us in what is not their original form, and scholars have made plausible conjectures regarding the documents that lie back of the Pentateuch and the Gospels. Moreover, it has been discovered that God's revelation took place to and through a nation set in the midst of other nations from which it sometimes borrowed freely. In all these ways the Bible has become a new book. Not yet have all the things we have learned about it been incorporated in our theology.

There is no use in saying that we do not like the changes thus forced upon us. The Church did not like it when John Wycliffe gave the English people a Bible they could understand, and the bishop did not like it when Tyndale proposed to translate the Greek New Testament. The pope did not like it when Martin Luther found out that the Bible of the Middle Ages had been corrupted and that the Scripture did not, as the Church long had taught, say, "Do penance," but rather, "Repent; change your mind; amend your lives." Regarding a fresh revelation of God's truth, the question never is whether we like it, but only how soon we shall make it a part of our life and thought.

In the midst of all this increase in learning, Jesus continues to stand first. The real marvel is that all the old manuscripts that have been found, all the fresh insights that have required adjustments in grammars and dictionaries, all the unearthing of information about Israel's neighbors and Christianity's rivals, do not in the slightest degree lessen the significance or undermine the authority of Jesus. The only change they effect in our attitude toward him is that we understand him better as his sayings are set over against their background and his words are seen to have been lifted from the common speech of the time and his character and being are disclosed to have been so unlike anything else that existed then or ever.

A theological seminary served the Church for three quarters of a century without a president, the senior professor acting as chairman of the faculty. Near the beginning of the present century, a Brooklyn pastor was chosen to be the president. He had no idea that he was being considered for such a position until a committee called on him to inform him of his election. He took that to be evidence of the divine will, and accepted.

In his inaugural address he discussed the hard work which, on the human side, had evidently gone into the creation of the Biblical literature. "Isaiah," he said, "worked over his prophetic roll before it became a climax of literature in his hands. The critics say that it took two of him to finish it. I could believe them if they said it took a dozen." Of the New Testament he said: "If criticism leaves me Christ, I have all I need. It does leave me Christ. . . . Now give me Christ and you give me Christianity."

Those who read the Scripture thus will find that it offers daily light and leading. Paul notified the Corinthians that it was only through Christ that the frequently read words of the law could really be understood. Of those not aware of this, he says: "To this day, when they read the old covenant, that same veil remains unlifted, because only through Christ is it taken away. Yes, to this day whenever Moses is read a veil lies over their minds; but when a man turns to the Lord the veil is removed" (II Cor. 3:14 f.). "Beyond the sacred page" he hears God speaking to him.

Sometimes the language used will have to be translated into our language. Jesus first spoke in the Palestinian tongue that he might be understood by Palestinians, just as he would have used an Eskimo dialect if he had been born in Alaska. No small part of Jonathan Edwards' ministry was devoted to translating into the language of New England what had first been spoken in the language of another land and another age. He was concerned to find the Bible's message for his own generation. When he denounced the practice of stealing fruit in Northampton, an objector cited a portion of Deut. 23:24: "When thou comest into thy neighbor's vineyard, then thou mayest eat grapes thy fill."

That indulgence was permitted in a land where vines abounded. The vineyards of the New England community were neither numerous nor luxuriant, and Edwards saw that a literal application of this passage would result in their swift and complete desolation. He noted that in Northampton apple orchards were about as plentiful as vineyards in Palestine. So, said he, "the liberty given in this text to the Children of Israel seems to be very parallel with the liberty taken among us, to take up an apple or two and eat as we are occasionally passing through a neighbor's orchard; which, as our circumstances are, we may justly do, and presume we have the owner's consent" (A. C. McGiffert, Jr., *Jonathan Edwards*, pages 114 f. Harper & Brothers, 1932).

It is in this spirit that the Bible provides help now in the midst of our perplexities. Visitors to Hampton Court, which is along the Thames, not far from London, will recall that this particular former royal residence is chiefly notable for its beautiful gardens and that in the gardens there is a maze. This maze consists of a baffling network of paths outlined by a very high hedge, a box-wood hedge considerably taller than a person. This hedge is planted in a pattern that is intricate indeed. It is a labyrinth which winds and twists and doubles back upon itself, and there are frequent dead ends.

The maze was first laid out a great many years ago — nobody knows quite why unless to amuse the ladies of the court, who probably had not much to do. Those who saw Emily Kimbrough and Cornelia Otis Skinner's autobiographical motion picture, *Our Hearts Were Young and Gay*, will recall the delightful scene that transpired there. The maze is of further interest because it was at Hampton Court that the men met who gave us the King James Version of the Bible.

For one penny now, one English penny, you can be admitted to the maze. You go through a turnstile and the trick is to find your way out again. You wind in and around, turn this way and that, and find yourself at some impasse. You wonder whether it is possible to reach the exit. There is a notice that the place closes at four o'clock. As the sun goes down you begin to get panicky, wondering why you came and whether you will ever see friends and loved ones again. The afternoon we were there, the paths were swarming with small boys, completely lost and thoroughly enjoying it — and determined that nobody would ever have to show them how to get out.

As for ourselves, we had no trouble at all in threading our way through the maze. We did not make a single wrong turning but accomplished the whole thing in the minimum of time and with the greatest of ease. This was due to the fact that we had the answer beforehand. This may not have been entirely fair, and we certainly did not intend to learn it in advance. We came upon it inadvertently. When we were reading the guidebook and planning our trip, there in black and white was the key to the maze, so simple and obvious that we could not go on pretending we had not seen it. The secret, says Baedeker, " is to turn to the right the first and second time that we have an option, and thereafter to the left." When you know that, it's easy — and once you know it you can't forget it.

This is the most famous maze in the world. Yet we do not have to journey to Hampton Court to get lost in a maze. The Bible is a maze, and we have noted some of the wrong turns, pitfalls, and dead ends which seem to hold such allure for so many. Life is a maze. Down every lane you come to a turning, and you don't know whether to go right or left. The walls of the lane are so high that you cannot see over, and the choice has to be made by faith rather than by sight. Sometimes you are sure you have made the right turn, only to find yourself in some blind alley, some dead end that leads nowhere. Sometimes after much twisting and turning you are sure you have made a great deal of progress — only to discover you are right back where you started.

But don't give up! There is no need for anybody to lie down and die. At Hampton Court the British Government has been characteristically thoughtful. Unseen at first, there is a guard who stands on a platform lofty enough to command a view of the entire scene. From his vantage point he can direct you to the exit, supplying from his omniscience what your own limited powers cannot attain. So also in life. Puzzling as it may be, it is not a hopeless maze. There is always the Guard on his platform, and

" behind the dim unknown,
standeth God within the shadow, keeping
watch above his own " (" The Present Crisis,"
James Russell Lowell. Used by permission of and arrange-

ment with the authorized publishers, Houghton Mifflin Company).

Best of all is the news that there is a key to the maze. At Hampton Court we got ours from Mr. Baedeker's well-known volume. In life, man's guidebook is the Bible. In the Bible, Jesus is the key to the whole. In any area of experience we must have some knowledge of the underlying plan before the meaning becomes clear. To get possession of the key to the riddle is to solve the problem or explain the project. The workers in a factory producing surgical instruments went about their tasks indifferently. They had not the remotest idea of the uses to which these tools were put. Then someone conceived the idea of taking the workers into operating theater. There they saw the surgeons at work, using the delicate tools they had made. Immediately they began to make better tools, and then asked the management to provide for them an entire course in human anatomy.

During World War II the Government took workmen into Army camps for a while, letting them see where their products went and why. Whoever writes a book knows that there must be an underlying theme which will tell him what to leave out and lend unity to what he puts in. Any musical composition has its theme, recurring at intervals, and our appreciation is enhanced if we know what that is. The French composer Widor was baffled by Bach's chorales until Albert Schweitzer explained their meaning. " I made the acquaintance," says Widor, " of a Bach of whose existence I had previously had only the dimmest suspicion." Everything became clear when he got the key to the maze.

Religion has sometimes been attacked on the ground of

its humble beginnings, in dread and superstition. Fear, it is alleged, created the gods, the idea of spirit originated from dreams, and the whole thing began in ignorance. We must allow anthropologists whatever latitude they desire for their investigations, but they ought to be reminded that great creations are not to be despised because they had humble beginnings. Before there were doctors, there were witch doctors, and the barber and the surgeon used to be one and the same. Will anyone on that account now refuse to go to the hospital when he has appendicitis?

Whatever the beginnings of religion, Jesus is the crown and climax of the process. A gospel that centers in him does not have to apologize for its origins. He lends meaning to the whole of the Scripture. A lad who in church school had studied some horror stories from the Old Testament observed that " God has changed a lot since Judges was written." God, of course, has not changed. He is the same " yesterday and today and for ever." Our ideas about him have changed since Jesus wholly revealed Him: " when the perfect comes, the imperfect will pass away."

When people raise as objections to the Christian religion the difficulty of believing that an axhead could float, or that bears would eat up children for taunting a prophet about his bald head, or that a man could live for three days in the stomach of a fish without being digested, we say that these are curious twists of the maze in which we must not get lost. They belong to the preparatory stage of religion and have, after all, nothing whatever to do with the fact that hope does not disappoint us, and the truth as it is in Christ sets us free, and love lasts on.

A British scientist said that science had taught him that " the most significant fact in the universe is process " — that is to say, it is going somewhere. He resolved to spend his life demonstrating what religion had taught him, namely, that " the most significant fact in the process is Jesus Christ." Here is a good place to begin our thinking about miracles. It used to be held that miracles were a proof of Christ's divinity. That is not Scriptural, for both Old and New Testaments attribute miracle-working powers to evil spirits as well as to good. Almost to the very end, the magicians of Pharaoh were able to duplicate the feats of Moses and Aaron. In II Thess. 2:9, Paul warns that the coming of " the lawless one " will be accompanied by " all power and with pretended signs and wonders."

If, therefore, people do not find it easy now to accept the miracles of Jesus as proof of his Messiahship, we need not urge it; rather should we go about it quite the other way around. The miracles do not explain Jesus; Jesus explains the miracles. Everything that science and psychology have disclosed confirms religion's conviction that the spirit is lord of the body. When you have a person like Jesus, whose mind and heart and purpose are entirely in accord with the mind and heart and purpose of God, then it would have been incredible if there had been no miracles. Life and health flowed out from him because with him were hid all the treasures of wisdom and knowledge.

It is God-in-Christ who makes sense of the mighty acts of redemption wrought during our Lord's last week on earth. The Gospels are fullest at that point. Mark has indeed been called the story of our Lord's Passion, with an introduction. The daily papers carried the story of a man in Florida who had been found hanging on a cross. Four-and-a-half-inch nails had been driven through his hands and his feet. The meaning of the incident was not entirely clear. The police surmised that he had staged the thing for the purpose of obtaining sympathy.

In any case, there is nobody who would offer that man as an explanation of the universe. There were two other crosses outside a city wall the afternoon our Lord was done to death, but it is only one of the three that is freighted with meaning for us. It is because our Lord lived the life he did that his death means what it does. His death avails because invariably he willed one will with God, who in him became partaker of our woe.

It is Jesus also who lends meaning to the doctrine of immortality. This is a doctrine that hardly becomes explicit in the Old Testament, yet it is mankind's oldest and most cherished belief. " The hope of immortality," said Plutarch, " and the hope of existence is the most venerable and the mightiest of all affections." If we want to see how old and venerable this hope is, we have but to visit the caves where anthropologists have found the earliest traces of human life. In the grave of Paleolithic man have been found the leg and foot bones of a wild ox — food supply for the great adventure — together with weapons and implements that had been of service; apparently these would be needed in the hereafter.

Ancient mothers sometimes buried their children beneath the earthen floor of home, so that they could never be far away. Some tribes of American Indians always bury a dog with a child, so that in the unfamiliar realm of spirits the child will always have a guide who can find the way home. Thus has man's oldest affection found embodiment. Thus has man expressed the conviction that he was not born to die. The hope has sometimes grown dim. About the time that Jesus came, the disillusionment and pessimism of the decadent Roman Empire showed itself in an epitaph that was so common that it was sometimes represented simply by the initial letters. The epitaph was this:

" I was not. I was. I am not. I do not care." Here, then, is confusion: on the one hand, persistent hope; on the other, world-weariness and despair.

Jesus is the key to this maze. It is evident that there is no human hope for which God has failed to provide fulfillment. Paul indeed says this is why the Bible was given to us: " Whatever was written in former days was written for our instruction, that by steadfastness and by the encouragement of the scriptures we might have hope" (Rom. 15:4). Man hopes for companionship – and God has richly endowed him with friends. Man hopes for the survival of his family – and God has blessed him with children. Man hopes for a revelation of the divine – and God has given him Jesus.

Paul argues that a God who has done that will fulfill our other hopes. " He who did not spare his own Son but gave him up for us all, will he not also give us all things with him? " (Rom. 8:32). When our friend has done many favors for us, we hesitate to ask him for another. The Biblical argument is quite the other way around. It is because God has done so much for us that we can confidently count on him yet to do more. Those whom we love have a habit of disclosing to us undreamed of qualities of truth and goodness. Jesus makes the best easily credible.

Revelation 19:10 declares that " the testimony of Jesus is the spirit of prophecy." That is to say, all that is of permanent worth in the prophetic Scriptures derives its value and power from the fact that it is preparatory to Christ. So also with the law. Christ made it clear that he had come to fulfill it. Keenly aware of the futility of trying to keep the law sufficiently to merit the favor of God, Paul declared that " Christ is the end of the law " (Rom. 10:4). So completely, however, does Christ fulfill and transform the old legalism that Paul elsewhere refers to "the law of Christ" (Gal. 6:2), which, as Augustine defined it, is to love God and do what you like.

Hearing that help is to be derived from Bible study, some distraught souls begin at the first chapter of Genesis, resolutely determined to read straight through to the end. They sometimes get bogged down in Leviticus, which, as Ronald Knox admits, no translator can ever make newsy. If they get past this, they seldom go beyond Numbers, parts of which read very much like the telephone book, and have approximately the same spiritual worth. Making a fresh start, they concentrate upon those passages in Exodus which indicate the punishment that is to be inflicted upon particular sins. It is a sense of guilt that has led them to the Bible in the first place. Exodus convinces them not only that they will be severely punished, but that their guilt will be inflicted upon generations yet unborn.

But all that has to be looked at in the light of what Jesus was and did. "Come to me," he says (Matt. 11:28), "all who labor and are heavy laden, and I will give you rest." He makes it clear that in a universe which has as creator a God who is Father we are not shut up to sin's inexorable consequences. There is a love that draws a veil over wrongdoing (cf. I Peter 4:8), and leads the wrongdoer, if he be penitent, out into the land of beginning again. "If we confess our sins, he is faithful and just, and will forgive our sins and cleanse us from all unrighteousness" (I John 1:9).

In February of 1919, Woodrow Wilson went to Raleigh, North Carolina, to make the address presenting a portrait of Stonewall Jackson to the Capitol Club. It was a gala occasion. The beauty and chivalry of the countryside were present for the annual ball. Preceding the dance, the World War President spoke briefly of the Civil War hero. He dwelt little on Jackson's military achievements. These, he said, were too well known to need comment. It was rather Jackson the Christian of whom he chose to speak, the Jackson for whom quiet trust in God was the dominant factor in life.

Then Mr. Wilson added his own confession. " I do not understand," he said, " how any man can approach the discharge of the duties of life without faith in the Lord Jesus Christ." A great hush fell upon the entire company, and no one thought of being gay until the President and his party had withdrawn. The incident still lingers in the memory of those who heard that confession of faith in that unusual circumstance. Even when seeking to know God's will in the Bible, we must come with such a life commitment.

It is important when using the Scripture to begin with Jesus. Read the stories about him, ponder his sayings, note the effect his presence had upon the diseased, the disturbed, and the dishonest. Note also what happened to those whose lives were touched by his. They banded themselves together for fellowship and then went everywhere preaching the glad good news. Then they turned to the Old Testament to find what sages and seers had written in ages long gone. New meaning they found wherever they looked.

Biologists tell us that the development of the individual recapitulates that of the race. So is it that the growth of man's spirit recapitulates the history of the Early Church. He begins with Christ. He feels his gracious welcome, his healing power, his forgiving love. He becomes a new creation. To understand all the hopes and history that culminated in Christ, he goes to the Old Testament. Christ's spirit gives him the measuring stick by which he decides what there is of permanent worth. That in turn lends new significance to the wondrous deeds wrought by God in Christ, through whom alone were " life and immortality " brought to light.